What Writers Read

What Writers Read

35 Writers on Their Favourite Book

Edited by
Pandora Sykes

BLOOMSBURY PUBLISHING
LONDON · OXFORD · NEW YORK · NEW DELHI · SYDNEY

BLOOMSBURY PUBLISHING
Bloomsbury Publishing Plc
50 Bedford Square, London, WC1B 3DP, UK
29 Earlsfort Terrace, Dublin 2, Ireland

BLOOMSBURY, BLOOMSBURY PUBLISHING and the Diana logo are trademarks
of Bloomsbury Publishing Plc

First published in Great Britain 2022

A catalogue record for this book is available from the British Library

ISBN: HB: 978-1-5266-5748-0; TPB: 978-1-5266-6038-1; EBOOK: 978-1-5266-5747-3;
EPDF: 978-1-5266-5746-6

2 4 6 8 10 9 7 5 3

Typeset by Newgen KnowledgeWorks Pvt. Ltd., Chennai, India
Printed and bound in Great Britain by CPI Group (UK) Ltd, Croydon CR0 4YY

To find out more about our authors and books visit www.bloomsbury.com
and sign up for our newsletters

'There is no friend as loyal as a book'

Ernest Hemingway

Contents

Contents

Contents

Pandora Sykes

Introduction

There is a newspaper slot that I love where authors are asked about the book they wish they had written, that made them laugh, that made them cry, and so on. I read it with a tab open on my favourite online second-hand bookshop, adding to my basket as I read. Knowing an author's favourite book feels like a delicious piece of insider information – like peeking behind their brain curtains to see the cogs turning within. It's highly unlikely that reading said book will confer a similar set of writing skills, but being in the same reading space that your favourite author has dwelt in is a lovely sort of alchemy. Why not create a whole book of moments like this? I thought. And so, here we are.

Over 413,000 children and young people in the UK don't own a book. This deprives them of education, but also of a means to escape: into a fantasy world from which they are able to better understand and navigate 'real' life. When I think of myself as a child, I think of myself on my own with a book, filling myself up with the energy to face the world. Alone, but never lonely. Children who have access to books are three times more likely to experience mental wellbeing as adults. Quite frankly, when I consider how much books have given me – and, at times, saved me – that feels like a conservative estimate.

All the profits and royalties from this book will go to the National Literacy Trust, which works to end literacy inequality. Nearly 800 public libraries have been shuttered in the last 10 years: safe, communal places where young people can gather, read, *be*. The decline in shared, free spaces is rarely front-page news, but that does not mean it is not an emergency. When we think of a library, we usually think of a huge, vaulted room with floor-to-ceiling books. But a library does not have to be enormous; research has found that just 80 books can make a child feel enriched. Through their Primary School Alliance, the National Literacy Trust aims to create 1,000 new libraries in primary schools, each with their own librarian, to curate and rotate the books. Working with local communities, they have also opened 'literary hubs' in lower-income communities across the UK. National Literacy

Trust hubs bring together local partners to tackle literacy issues in communities across the UK where low levels of literacy are seriously impacting on people's lives.

The beauty of these 35 entries that you are about to read – or dip into whenever you have a few spare minutes on the loo/in the bath/in bed before nodding off, which is how I very much hope this book will be consumed, with its pages water-wrinkled and stained with peanut butter – is the specific personal detail that each author brings. Elif Shafak writes about the solace and freedom she found in Virginia Woolf's fluid *Orlando* as a young bisexual woman growing up in conservative Turkey. Nick Hornby writes about escaping into Erich Kästner's *Emil and the Detectives* aged 11, as his father prepared to leave the family home for his other family. Marian Keyes writes about the book that lifted her when she was suicidal. Emma Dabiri marvels at how changed you can find yourself as a reader, to return to a book you were bored by 12 years earlier, and find it so nourishing, so personally resonant.

It was important to me that these contributions are not book reports (there's Goodreads for that), but a snapshot into the writer as a person, told through the book that they were reading at that time. Some of these entries, such as Lisa Taddeo on the book she read during the emotional rollercoaster of first postpartum hangover, will make you laugh out loud. Others, like George the Poet on Malcolm Gladwell's influence on the social-academia of his award-winning poetry, will make you think. Some resisted my brief, by which I was delighted: Fatima Bhutto wrote about a bookshelf of books, because it is a fool's errand to choose one.

I know what she means. I wrote the brief, so I should surely plant my flag in the sand, but when I think about the books that changed me, my mind crowds with about 10 different highly specific instances. On my single bed aged 10, in floods of tears, reading *Goodnight Mister Tom* by Michelle Magorian. On a bus aged 17, shivering, as I got to the twist in *We Need To Talk About Kevin* by Lionel Shriver. In a writing hut, ignoring my book deadline, gobbling *When I Hit You* by Meena Kandasamy over one long insomniac night.

I have a reputation for reading the 'wrong' thing at the 'wrong' time: the girthy *Riders* by Jilly Cooper in RE class at my all-girls convent school; Leïla Slimani's gut-punching *Lullaby* whilst heavily pregnant with my first child. (For her contribution to this anthology, Leïla has written about another

4

book that cracked open my teenage brain like a walnut: *The Unbearable Lightness of Being* by Milan Kundera.) I like reading 'a frothy summer read' in the dead of winter and 'a serious work of non-fiction' on a sun lounger. Books should not be siloed into times of year or personality types. Reading widely benefits all of us, but it should not be didactic. What you enjoy should not be filtered or apologised for. Quite frankly, life is too short to force yourself to finish a book – or to stop yourself returning to a favourite. (Surreally, I was re-reading David Nicholls's *One Day* for possibly the tenth time when his entry landed in my inbox.)

A friend of mine recently remarked upon how 'starry' the list was, with its prizewinners and shortlisted authors. It's true that many of these writers are bona fide literary stars – and I am still in shock that they all agreed to write a piece, entirely for free, despite their calendars and status. But in this collection, they are simply readers. To go one further, they are writers *because* they are readers. Which is why we must think of the next generation of readers, many of whom are growing up without as much access to books. As Margaret Atwood said last year, 'If there are no young readers and writers, there will shortly be no older ones. Literacy will be dead, and democracy – which many believe goes hand in hand with it – will be dead as well.'

Thank you for buying a copy of this book and supporting the great work of the National Literacy Trust. I hope you enjoy what you find.

Nick Hornby

on *Emil and the Detectives* by Eric Kästner

I turned 11 in April 1968, which was around the time the wheels came off the family car. They were already pretty loose. My father was one of those 1960s men who, in the pre-digital crossed-line age of phoneboxes and busy signals and telegrams in an emergency, managed to start a second family without the first one knowing anything about it. When the truth was revealed (not to everyone – it would be another four or five years before my sister and I discovered that we had half-siblings), that wasn't the end of the calamity. The First Family, or three-quarters of it, had to move house in the new belt-tightening regime, but there was a short period between houses, maybe a couple of months, that was partly spent in what might have been called a pensione if it had been in Italy rather than on the outskirts of Maidenhead, and partly spent in the house of a family friend who already had three children of her own.

It was there and then that I got sick, quite badly, with hepatitis, and I missed a term of school. (It was this term, I'm guessing, where I missed out on *Vanity Fair* and *War and Peace* and every other book I should have read but haven't.) When I was well enough to eat and drink, I lived off Lucozade and Twiglets and nothing else. But right at the beginning of the illness, when I was feverish and a little hallucinatory, I started to become extremely worried about Emil Tischbein's missing money and to express that worry out loud, several times.

Emil Tischbein was the hero of Erich Kästner's great children's book, *Emil and the Detectives*. I had read the book for the first time a couple of years before, and I suspect I had reread it for comfort when I was merely feeling under the weather and in bed, before the nasty stuff kicked in. Like many people of my generation, I read a lot when I was a kid, not because I was a swot but because I loathed and feared being bored, and the 1960s and 1970s were boring times for kids: two television channels worth watching, neither of them showing anything during the day, no live sport, nothing open at all on Sundays, no games apart from the board games that Henry VIII had probably played: Snakes & Ladders, Mouse Trap and so on. I chose to read authors who had written hundreds of books that were exactly the same – Captain W. E. Johns and the Biggles books, Enid Blyton with her Fives and Sevens, Anthony Buckeridge and Jennings, Charles Hamilton's Billy Bunter, Pamela Lyndon Travers' *Mary Poppins*. My mother took us to the library every Saturday morning, and on finding a likely candidate for borrowing, I would check the page listing the author's publications. If there weren't 20 or 30 books listed with almost identical titles, I wouldn't bother. I hadn't heard of Harper Lee, but I'd have needed a lot more from her before she could have persuaded me to take out *To Kill A Mockingbird*. I would have needed her to kill most of the birds in North America at a rate of one a year.

I don't know how *Emil and the Detectives*, or Erich Kästner, sneaked through. There was a sequel, but only one, and I have only discovered recently, on an idle googling afternoon, that Kästner wasn't really a children's book author at all. He was a satirist and a poet and a scriptwriter, he was nominated for the Nobel six times, he was a German pacifist during World War II and he had his books burned by the Nazis in 1933. Yet, he wrote the immortal Emil and another undisputed classic: *Lottie and Lisa*, which you may know better through one of the two versions of the movie *The Parent Trap*, starring Hayley Mills and then Lindsay Lohan. Kästner was quite a guy.

I think one can tell that *Emil and the Detectives* is a children's book written by someone who wasn't a children's writer most of the time. The plot takes the form of an adventure: Emil's mother, a widow, sends him from the provinces to Berlin to stay with his aunt and grandmother while she works. He travels on his own on the train and falls asleep. When he wakes up, the money that his mother had provided for the trip – at great personal cost – has disappeared from the lining of his jacket, where Emil had hidden it. When he arrives in Berlin at the wrong station, he falls in with a gang of kids who help him find the thief.

But this is a children's book where everything seems real. Real and a little bit sad, despite the familiar form and Walter Trier's beautiful, optimistic illustrations. There is no innocent explanation: the thief is a thief. The money is felt, by the reader and the characters, as a devastating loss. The effect is like a bad dream, where each step takes Emil further and further from where he wants to be. It's no wonder, really, that a sick boy would hallucinate it.

When a writer looks back on their cultural consumption, you can make an argument that everything that was swallowed up was important and influential in some way. But there are some books that you know are there, at the core of you; I have never had to be reminded of *Emil and the Detectives*. I think I still have my original copy – I certainly own a paperback of *Lottie and Lisa* with Hayley Mills on the cover. Why did that children's book climb above all the others? Maybe the realism? I try not to write about things that don't seem real to me. Maybe the sense that this was a defining moment in a character's life? None of my characters have returned for another defining moment. Maybe the combination of humour and sadness, a mixture important to me as a writer and a reader? But this is me trying to talk myself into making a case for my discovery of Kästner's lovely novel as a crucial step on my professional journey. I suspect it provided something much more than that: comfort, distraction and companionship at a time when I was struggling badly. And you can't ask for more from a book than that.

Nick Hornby is a British writer and screenwriter and the author of eight novels, including About A Boy *and* High Fidelity, *and eight works of non-fiction including* Fever

Nick Hornby

Pitch, *all of which have been adapted for screen to acclaim. He has won an Emmy for his TV series,* State of the Union, *and two of his screenplays,* An Education *and* Brooklyn, *have been nominated for Oscars.*

Monica Ali

on *Pride and Prejudice* by Jane Austen

It is a truth universally acknowledged that a brilliant novel may forever be ruined by being forced to read it at school. But my first encounter with *Pride and Prejudice* took place in a classroom, and it ignited my lifelong love affair with Austen's work.

Every time I come back to *Pride and Prejudice*, I find something different in it depending on where I am in my life. When I first read it as an adolescent, I related to Lizzie's agonies of embarrassment over her family. I think that's wonderful and deeply telling – that despite the centuries, class and culture that separated me from Austen's protagonist, I related to and drew strength from her inner struggles. In another reading, this time shortly after I had started my own family, I became acutely aware of the narrow, domestic gaze of the novel. The big world – the

Napoleonic wars, the stirrings of the industrial revolution – barely features in Austen's work. She gives us the world in a bowl of white soup. And the work gains greatly in intensity and beauty.

From feeling frustrated and trapped beneath a breastfeeding infant, I began to appreciate that what is important is not what you see, but how – and how carefully – you see it. More recently, while writing my novel *Love Marriage*, what I drew from another rereading was that while Austen writes about courtship, engagements and marriage, the reader actually does learn a great deal about how the society of the time worked. Austen is very sharp in her observations about money, power, class and the position of women. I drew inspiration from that in my own writing, using the rituals and customs and family dynamics surrounding an impending wedding as a lens to look at how we live and love in Britain today.

Pride and Prejudice has spawned so many imitators that sometimes it feels, in a way, damned by its own success. Can any book that popular be truly worthwhile? Okay, so it gave us Colin Firth in a wet shirt in the television adaptation, and many of us are enduringly grateful for that. But doesn't that just emphasise the shallowness of the novel's appeal?

Of the widespread affection for this book there can be no doubt. On the many Jane Austen websites – the Republic of Pemberley, for example – the most ardent discussions are reserved for *Pride and Prejudice*. The book has spawned an entire film and television industry, including *Bride and Prejudice*, a Bollywood reworking that speaks to the universality of the themes. And there have been sequels written and much homage paid, not least of which is Bridget Jones.

So, am I just a hopeless romantic, sucked into the well-told, romantically idealised tale of Lizzie, who is resolute in her goal of marrying, against the odds, for love?

Absolutely not.

'It is a truth universally acknowledged that a single man in possession of a good fortune must be in want of a wife.' Austen's exquisite irony lays bare the institution of marriage as an exchange commodity system. Yet she treats the subject with a great deal of subtle inflection, making a thorough study of the married state, from the unequal union of Mr and Mrs Bennet, through the unstable passion of Lydia and Wickham, to Charlotte's marriage to the gruesomely pompous and obsequious Mr Collins. Lizzie's initial response to her friend's decision is one of horror. But it is part of Elizabeth's maturation that she comes to admire Charlotte's ability to manage her household and her husband, whose many silly statements 'Charlotte wisely did not hear'.

Of course, Elizabeth Bennet is a character I love. Quick-witted, lively, self-assured, full of good sense and yet so fallibly human. It is not only her prejudices she must conquer to make the match with Darcy but, to some extent, her pride. She is ruled by reason, but she makes mistakes. Austen gives us the landscape of her internal conflicts with a level of psychological insight that still seems both acute and fresh today.

Other heroines may stand up to and even conquer domineering men of so-called higher standing, others yet may represent our fears or wish-fulfilment fantasies, but Elizabeth takes the reader on her most important journey – and it's not the one to Pemberley but the path to self-knowledge. And that's why I'm among the many millions of her adoring fans.

Monica Ali is a British-Bangladeshi author of five novels, including Brick Lane *and* Love Marriage. *A Fellow of the Royal Society of Literature, she has been nominated for the Booker Prize, the George Orwell Prize and the Critics' Circle Award and has taught creative writing at Columbia University, New York.*

Ann Patchett

on *Sorrow and Bliss* by Meg Mason

Back in the days when I was just a novelist, as opposed to a novelist who owns a bookshop, I favoured dead writers. When people asked who had shaped me, I would trot out Mann and Garcia Marquez and Welty.

Then we opened Parnassus Books and everything changed. The dead still get plenty of real estate in bookshops, but they get very little of the booksellers' attention. That's because we're endlessly pummelled by the new books coming out. Every week a crop of titles is set loose on the world and the booksellers scramble to read as much as possible so that we can converse intelligently with our customers. I'd like to read Dickens again, but I doubt I will until I sell the store.

Because I am a bookshop owner who is also a novelist, everyone wants to send me their books. Not only can I write catchy endorsements, I can also actually press the book into customers' hands. I receive rafts of advance reading copies, busloads and boatloads of books I'll never have time to read. I understand this is a luxury, but sometimes I forget.

I read and read. I had just sent in a quote for a very good first novel called *Valentine* by Elizabeth Wetmore. I picked it for our store's first editions club. I was pleased to give the editor the good news.

But a not a week went by before that same editor was back again saying she was very sorry, but would I please take a look at this other new book because she thought I'd like it, too.

When there are a hundred people asking for a favour, the person I am least inclined to help is the person I just finished helping. Didn't this editor know I was being crushed to death by fiction? Plus the author of this new book lived in Australia, which meant I couldn't pick the title for my book club even if I wanted to (we need signed copies). Worse still, the cover indicated a kind of lady fiction I don't go for.

I had just taken the recycle bin to the kerb five minutes before. Instead of throwing the book on the towering pile of books I'll never get to, I decided to walk it straight to the bin. I opened to the first page while walking down the stairs. I stopped in the driveway. I turned the page.

I stood in the driveway for five pages. Then the book and I went back inside.

Meg Mason's novel *Sorrow and Bliss* is an impossible rarity: a book of profound emotional depth that makes the reader bark like a seal. The world is full of books capable of scaring me to death or moving me to tears. There are no end of titles that can educate me in matters I know nothing about. But books that make me laugh out loud are rare. A book that, when read in bed, will make my husband say, 'What's so funny?' and then when I tell him, he'll laugh too, those books are scarce. But were I to try to find a book that is funny and also scares me and moves me and educates me, *Sorrow and Bliss* would be standing by itself.

I won't tell you what the book is about because I want you to read it the way I read it: in a driveway, open to amazement. I will, however, tell you what I wrote for the jacket: '*Sorrow and Bliss* is a brilliantly faceted and extremely funny book that engulfed me in the way I'm always hoping to be engulfed by novels. While I was reading it, I was making a list of all the people I wanted to send it to, until I realized that I wanted to send it to everyone I know.'

By the time the hardbacks arrived at the bookshop, we were deep in the pandemic. Many

19

people had told me they were having trouble reading. 'I want something funny,' customers said. 'I want a book that will hold my attention and not let me go. I want a book that will make me feel smart and not crush me at the end.'

I had just what they were looking for.

We ordered cases of *Sorrow and Bliss*. We ordered busloads. We sold them all.

Did this book change my life? Yes, but in an unexpected way. Meg Mason wrote to me from Australia to thank me, and I wrote back to thank her. Those letters led to an exchange of emails, then phone calls, then Zooms, then voice notes, then friendship. A true friend is always an agent of change. What luck it is to love someone you've never met, to be elevated and improved by both the author and her book.

Ann Patchett is an American writer and the owner of Parnassus Books, an independent bookstore in Nashville. She is the author of eight novels, including Bel Canto, *and five works of non-fiction, including* This Is the Story of a Happy Marriage. *She has been awarded a PEN/ Faulkner Award and the Women's Prize for Fiction.*

Leïla Slimani

on *The Unbearable Lightness of Being* by Milan Kundera

I was 14 years old. It was the summer of 1995 and we'd installed ourselves at our house in Kabila, a small village on the Mediterranean coast in the north of Morocco. During the holidays, my parents would go out a lot and have friends over often. I loved watching them drink, laugh and dance. I loved eavesdropping on adult conversations that I didn't totally understand. That summer, my mother was reading a book with a beige cover, decorated with the famous red border of *La Nouvelle Revue Française*. Its title: *The Unbearable Lightness of Being*. She brought it everywhere with her. When we went shopping, she'd rest it on her naked thighs whilst driving. The unbearable lightness of being? What could that possibly mean? It was an incantation that had a strange effect on me. I asked my mother what it was about. She said: 'It's a very beautiful book but I wouldn't know how to summarise it.'

One afternoon, my parents went out on a boat trip. I've always had seasickness and I decided to stay home alone. I lay down on the bed, opened the book at random and here's what I read: 'He undressed her, during which time she was almost inert. When he kissed her, her lips did not respond. Then she suddenly noticed she was moist and was appalled. She felt excitement, which was all the greater, given it was despite herself.'

I was physically overwhelmed by this chapter. For the first time in my life, literature had provoked a sensual, erotic shock in me. I think I blushed, closed the book and ran back to my room. That night, and during the days that followed, I did not stop thinking about it. And then, one day, I stole the book. I pretended to be sick and locked myself in my room. I remember it was very hot out. There was sand on the sheets of my bed and notes of music resonated in the air outside. People were having a party, somewhere.

The story unfolds in Prague at the end of the 1960s. Tomas is a surgeon who divorced 10 years earlier after a brief marriage, the remains of which include few memories and a son. He's a polygamist at heart who cannot conceive of another emotion than erotic friendship. He makes an exception for Tereza, a waitress in a brasserie who shows up in his life and attaches herself to him for two weeks by way of a very nasty bout of flu. At night, Tomas holds her hand to help her fall asleep. He loves her but cannot stop cheating on her, notably with Sabrina, a painter who walks around her atelier naked, dressed only in her father's bowler hat.

Their lives are suddenly disrupted by the arrival of Russian tanks in Prague and the repression that ensues. Tomas wonders about the responsibility of Czech communists: if they pretend not to see what's going on does that make them innocent? He publishes an extremely critical article that his superior asks him to renounce. He refuses, so the couple must emigrate to Zurich, only to eventually return to Prague. Banned from practising medicine, Tomas becomes a window washer, then a truck driver, pursued all the while by the Russian police force.

At the time I first read it, I was living in Morocco under the regime of Hassan II and there was no freedom of expression. My own father would end up in prison, accused of a crime he did not commit. Through the magic of literature, I discovered unexpected similarities between communist Prague and my own country. It was during this period that I discovered my passion for Central Europe. I read Zweig, Kafka, Márai, Kertész, and at the age of 22, I moved to Budapest for a couple of months.

I have reread this book dozens of times. My copy is dog-eared and annotated, and I think I'd endure a great deal of sorrow were I one day to lose it. Certain scenes have made a lifelong impression on me. It is impossible to sum this book up. One could say it's a novel about love, or rather, the inability to love, to be at once faithful to another and to oneself. This story also has a philosophical dimension and each situation provides the narrator with a chance to wonder about the human condition. If we only live once, why stubbornly insist on favouring severity?

I don't know what I really understood at the time. And deep down I tell myself it's not what matters most. It's less about 'understanding' a novel than being understood by it. It's a total book and a liberated book in which Kundera invents his own style. This novel achieves the most incredible literary fusion, blending myth, love story, musical score and political reflection. And it's this liberty that creates a reading experience that is at once intellectual and sensual.

My first novel, *In the Garden of the Ogre*, is an homage to Kundera's work. Adele, the main character, reads *The Unbearable Lightness of Being* and is blown away. When my book was published, I sent a copy to Milan Kundera. A few weeks later, I received a letter at home. It contained a drawing of the Czech author and this note: 'Thank you for your novel. Milan.'

Leïla Slimani is a Franco-Moroccan journalist and the author of four novels, including Chanson Douce, *which won the Prix Goncourt, the most prestigious literary award in France. It was published in the UK in 2016 as* Lullaby *and won a British Book Award. In 2017, she was appointed representative for the 'promotion of French language and culture' by Emmanuel Macron.*

David Nicholls

on *The Pan Book of Horror Stories* selected by Herbert van Thal

Of all the milestones on the journey into adulthood, the acquisition of a full library card was the one I craved the most. I was in no great hurry to join the armed forces or get married, but the library considered me a grown-up, rather generously, at 13, and there'd be no more sitting on bean bags, reading books with pictures. At 13, I'd be downstairs with the big boys, browsing through the forbidden fruit, the vinyl library, *Jaws*, the Shirley Conrans and Stephen Kings. At 13, I would finally have access to *The Pan Book of Horror Stories: Volume Two*.

It was the cover that grabbed me; an ivy-tangled hand emerges from a fresh grave – thrilling enough in itself, except the palm of the hand contains a fresh human eyeball. An eyeball! I knew that it was a mistake to judge a book by its cover but how could this be anything less than phenomenal? *Volume Four* featured a tarantula crawling across a sinister china doll, *Volume Five* showed a skull wearing a bobbed wig for no very clear reason, each volume compiled by someone called Herbert van Thal, editor and lord of darkness. A teenage horror freak, I tore through each edition with the same commitment that kept me in front of the TV until midnight to watch *Tales from the Crypt* and *The Blood on Satan's Claw*.

The short story is a famously delicate and sophisticated form, more poetry than prose, though this was not necessarily the case with *Volume Eight* (centipede crawling out of skull's eye socket). At 13, it was all about The Twist, which usually involved someone being buried alive or the narrator being revealed as a vampire. The success or failure of a short story was entirely proportional to the unpredictability and unpleasantness of this final narrative flourish, and even now, reading the filigreed miniatures of Alice Munro or Katherine Mansfield, a small part of me is waiting for the protagonist to be impaled or torn apart by cats or sent spinning into infinite space.

The late 1970s and early 1980s were the golden age of sleazy horror, of the X-certificate and the video nasty, but books somehow slipped under the radar. The most highly prized contraband was the work of James Herbert, who I revered, read and reread so that even now if you were to hand me a copy of *The Fog* or *The Rats*, I could quickly direct you to the most gruesome scenes. Dickens aside, Herbert was the only author I would recognise on the street. Warlock hair, a leather blouson with the sleeves rolled up, the bass player from an Iron Maiden tribute band, he had us all in his grip, inspiring a whole genre of cheap pulpy fiction in which innocuous branches of the animal kingdom are exposed to radiation and develop a taste for human flesh, because that's what radiation does. In *Night of the Crabs*, it was giant, sadistic crabs, in *Slugs,* it was – well, you get the idea. Did I really read a book called *Earthworms?* I have a feeling that I did.

But, like the Pan anthologies, I can't really remember much of it now. If I'm nostalgic for anything, it's not the writing, which became increasingly salacious, reactionary and sadistic as the series wore on. But I do remember vividly the experience of reading, the pull the stories had, their ability to steal sleep and make my heart beat faster. It was fiction as a fairground ride, shallow and disreputable but still thrilling. I'm aware that this sounds more like a confession than a celebration and perhaps it might have been more impressive to write about Turgenev's melancholy or first encounters with *The Waste Land*, rather than stories in which, more often than not, people were eaten alive from the inside by frogs. Looking back now through the list of contributors, I realise that these books were my first exposure to writers that I'd go on to love. Muriel Spark is in there and Dahl of course, but also Ray Bradbury, Patricia Highsmith, Ian McEwan and even William Faulkner. Which isn't to make any great literary claims for the Pan books; the lettuce doesn't turn a burger into salad.

But perhaps it's futile to separate out the nutritious and improving from the excessive and unhealthy. Whatever their source, the words go in and become part of who we are, and while I can't remember every part of the process, it really isn't that great a leap from Poe to Robert Louis Stevenson to Dickens to the Brontës, from H. G. Wells to that other rat enthusiast George Orwell, or perhaps across the Atlantic to Vonnegut and Stephen King, to Shirley Jackson and Margaret Atwood, all these authors made easily available to me, free of charge, through the public library system.

Neither do I think it's a coincidence that this obsession started when I was 13. Adolescence is its own horror story and in some indefinable way, I'm sure there was some release there from the

angst and tension of double chemistry followed
by games that all too often could feel like that
scene in *The Fog,* the scene with the PE teacher
and the kids, that bit where . . .

Well, you'll have to read it yourself. I'll lend
you my copy. Be warned though, it's really, truly
horrible.

*David Nicholls is a British novelist and screenwriter, best
known for the sliding-doors love story* One Day, *which
has been translated into 40 languages and has sold five
million copies worldwide. The author of five novels, he
has adapted several books for screen, including Edward St
Aubyn's Patrick Melrose series, for which he was nominated
for an Emmy and a BAFTA.*

Benjamin Zephaniah

on *Ain't I a Woman* by bell hooks

I came to London in late 1978. I was an angry, political and energetic 21-year-old from Birmingham, trying to get away from gangsterism and gun culture and wanting to make a name for myself as a poet. I'd started speaking poetry from a really young age, five or six. I didn't call it poetry, I called it playing with words. I inherited this love of words from my mother, who was part of the oral tradition. My mother never read a novel, but she spoke many. I was the same. I'd left school at 13, and I could hardly read or write, but I could speak novels.

I'd not long come from Birmingham when I walked into a café and bookshop in Stratford called Page One Books. They'd been given a grant from the Arts Council to publish books from under-represented communities. I turned up one day saying, I'm a poet, can you publish me? People didn't understand performance poetry then. They would say, we don't get rap poetry, we don't get Jamaican poetry, we don't know what to do with it. I'd had a lot of rejection, but this cooperative said they'd publish me on one condition: I had to join the collective. I said, all right. It was a bit hippy and alternative. We all ate, lived and worked together – even shared bicycles and a car.

Page One Books had lots of books on politics and a massive section of feminist literature. There were a lot of hardcore feminists in the collective. I remember, once, I got told off because I was singing 'Once, Twice, Three Times A Lady'. 'What's this lady thing, anyway!?' one said. They taught me that a woman being 'as good as a man' or 'as bad as a man' isn't feminism. That real feminism is liberation for men as well as women.

There is no getting around it, I was raised sexist. The things that the men around me told me about women are things that I completely disagree with now, but at the time I thought, all right. These were upstanding men of the community, respected men, who taught me a misogynistic idea of what men think and how women are. But something deep inside me thought, this can't be right. My twin sister can't be less of a human being than me. We were born of the same mother at the same time. What I learned in the collective was so essential and so grounding. Forty years later, I'm still friends with some of them.

The best thing about working in the bookshop is that any book I wanted to read, I could read. One day, I picked up *Ain't I a Woman* by bell hooks. There'd been a lot of talk about that book in the Black community. One of the things I love about the book is that it doesn't really have soundbites. bell tells the story of women from back in the 17th century, right up until the present day, or up until 1981 when the book was published. The book made me realise something really important. Black men have a raw deal. White women have a raw deal. So a Black woman? Well, think about the deal that *they* get.

When I read it, it challenged me in many ways, and even now, every time I read or listen to it, I learn more. I listened to it as an audiobook recently, while driving on tour, and I had these moments of, *Oh I get that bit now*. It's me growing as a person. bell hooks always said she wrote the book to appeal to people like me, who weren't brilliantly educated.

bell is also very critical of some of my heroes, like James Baldwin, Malcolm X and Martin Luther King. And she's right, these men don't say much about women. I had read their books, so why didn't I notice that they didn't talk about women? Is it because I am a man too, or is it because I've put them on a pedestal? I found these men so inspiring but when I read what bell had written about the women's organisation in the civil rights movement and even how people like my other hero, Angela Davis, were marginalised in the movement, it really had an effect on me. I realised that the Black Panther movement was sexist.

I recommend *Ain't I a Woman* to everyone. But I also say, prepare to be challenged. That's not a bad thing. I love being challenged. I'm always happy to say I've made mistakes. I've read a lot of Indian philosophy, and I've studied martial arts, and they have taught me to strive to get rid of the ego. Whatever you see me doing in the public arena doesn't come from my education at Oxford or Cambridge or Eton. It comes from my life experience. It comes from reading bell hooks in Page One Books.

Benjamin Zephaniah is a British-Jamaican poet, writer, actor, broadcaster and musician, who has written over 40 plays, poetry collections, works of non-fiction and books for children and young adults. Professor of Poetry and Creative Writing at Brunel University, he has been awarded numerous honorary doctorates. He has presented dozens of shows for television and radio including Life & Rhymes, *which won a BAFTA.*

Elizabeth Strout

on *The Pink Maple House* by Christine Noble Govan

When I was in the third grade, I had a teacher called Miss Lurvy. She seemed old to me, and she probably was – it was rumoured that she had taught a classmate's grandfather, but who knows. One day, Miss Lurvy said to the boy who sat in front of me – he never spoke; he was very poor, and no one ever spoke to him – Miss Lurvy walked up to him and said in front of the class, 'You have dirt behind your ears. No one is too poor to buy a bar of soap.' The poor boy's neck became terribly red as I watched from behind. He still did not speak. I have written and talked of this before, and I used it in *My Name is Lucy Barton*.

But Miss Lurvy liked me. One day she brought me over to the 'library' in the room, which was three small shelves of books, and she told me I could find one book and take it home to read.

This was considered an honour. The book I found was *The Pink Maple House*.

This book made a huge and lasting impression on me. It was about a friendship between two girls in the third grade. One girl – Polly – moves to another town, and so the two girls can't go to school together any more, but her friend, Jenny, comes and visits Polly all the time. And their life is perfect. Polly's mother is perfect, and her father is perfect and even Jenny's parents turn out to be perfect. So why did I love this book so much back then?

Because of the girl Tilly, who is at the new school, and Tilly is very poor and sleeps on the sofa with no room of her own, and for a while the two perfect girls are mean to Tilly, but then Polly's mother speaks to them about her, and they become nice to her.

I have used Tilly also in *My Name is Lucy Barton*.

I suspect the reason I loved that book so much was because I had a very good friend at that time, and to my eyes, her mother was perfect. (It turned out there were serious problems in that house.) But to my mind, back then this mother was kind and pretty and always so good to us. My mother was different. And so I must have felt split between Tilly and the girl Polly, I must have inhabited both their worlds as I read that book.

And I also remembered that poor boy who Miss Lurvy spoke of so meanly that day about his dirty ears. I think this book was probably the first time in my unfolding consciousness that I understood class differences. With no name for it, of course.

I recently bought this book and looked through it again. Polly's mother had a woman who 'helped with the laundry' and that would have gone straight over my head as a third grader; I knew nobody who had help like that. But Tilly stayed in my mind – in fact, hers was the only name I remembered – and as I look through the book now, it seems almost saccharine to me, the perfection of the girls' lives versus Tilly's life. But it is Tilly I always remembered. She had no room of her own and slept on the sofa, and while I had a room of my own, it was never heated.

The point is: Tilly, with her unattractive mother, was unforgettable to me, and also the girls' attitude towards her until Polly's nice mother made them be kind to her – and they were.

It would be wonderful if life was really like this, but it is not. Still, it was a kind of awakening for me. I have remembered it – and even used it in my work – after all these years.

Elizabeth Strout is an American author of eight novels, including My Name Is Lucy Barton *and* Olive

Kitteridge, *which won a Pulitzer and was later turned into a TV series for HBO, starring Frances McDormand. In 2022, she was elected to the American Academy of Arts and Letters.*

Sara Collins

on *Bridget Jones's Diary* by Helen Fielding

I was 21 when I started reading *Bridget Jones's Diary*. I remember the moment vividly. I was taking my baby to her babysitter's house before work. It was a really hellish route involving two buses, a train and a tube, and I always felt especially sorry for myself when I had to wake up at 4.30am to start it. It was one of those periods in my life when I was feeling like I hadn't lived up to other people's expectations for me. I'd always done well in school and had long been expected to follow in my dad's barrister footsteps. However, I had found out I was pregnant during law school and was at the time raising my daughter as a single mum while doing my pupillage. All of this had been a bit of a wrinkle in the path that had been laid out for me. I was feeling that keenly when I picked up this book.

Bridget Jones's Diary was exactly the book I needed, at the very moment I needed it. It was as if Bridget herself had sat down beside me on the bus and started whispering in my ear about her insecurities and secrets. I think the best novels make you feel like you are gaining access to a real person's secret self. Because this one takes the form of a diary, it is not only confessional, but also immediate; you feel as if you are living each mortifying, hilarious moment with Bridget. Here was the type of companionship I'd looked for every time I read, ever since I read my first book to myself aged three. That day, Bridget joined the pantheon of my literary friends, which included Jo March, Jane Eyre, Elizabeth Bennet. But each of them was, let's face it, a bit of a goody two shoes. Bridget was the messy heroine of her own life, which was how I had to start seeing myself.

The best novels are also a record of time and place. *Bridget Jones's Diary* is a love letter to London – which I love because I love London. It is a state-of-the-nation-in-the-mid-90s novel. In her bonkers efforts at self-improvement, Bridget tries to become more learned about current events, which, rereading the novel nowadays, might be a bit like reading historical fiction for women younger than I am, but I suppose what makes it timeless is the way it explodes the myth of perfection that so many women struggle with.

When I finished the novel for the first time, I promptly forgot its lessons. That's the thing about lessons – they are of limited use when you're young. For a good 20 years afterwards, I struggled with the myth of perfection in my personal and professional life, thinking I had to become a partner in a law firm, kitted out in power suits and stilettos, looking like the kind of woman who can do it all. But it was miles away from how I was feeling inside and from what I really wanted to do. I had ignored the message of Bridget: you have to find a way of being happy with being yourself. It took a creative writing course in 2014, after my youngest child started high school, to find my way back.

Bridget Jones's Diary changed the zeitgeist in ways that I think we are still exploring today. I trace a lot of the stuff that I've been obsessed with recently, like *Killing Eve* and *Fleabag*, to Bridget Jones's brand of truthfulness. In my own book, *The Confessions of Frannie Langton*, I also tried to evoke a confessional tone (I suppose it is also a diary of sorts) and to engage with a truthful way of looking at Britain's colonial history.

There are, of course, things that were acceptable in the 1990s that we wouldn't tolerate now. But I think a lot of *Bridget Jones's Diary* remains true today, even if we don't like to think that's the case. We have a tendency nowadays to curate our imperfections. We've all been liberated, rightfully and delightfully so, by the ideas of body positivity, but deep down we still have the same foibles and quirks and worries about 'how do I look?' and 'who's in love with me?' and 'am I doing well in my work?' and 'are my friends ignoring me?' So, it still comes full circle to the idea that there is a gap between who we show the world and who we really are.

For me, the joy of reading is that books forge these connections between the unlikeliest of people. There was a lot about Bridget's life that bore no resemblance to mine as a young Caribbean single mum, but there was a lot we had in common also. Bridget is a character conjured up by another woman's imagination, yet she electrified mine – I think that's magic. It'd be wonderful to meet Helen Fielding to be able to tell her how much her novel meant to me.

Sara Collins is a Caymanian-British writer, screenwriter and former lawyer. Her 2016 debut novel, The Confessions of Frannie Langton, *won the Costa First Novel Award. She is currently adapting her novel for screen.*

Tessa Hadley

on *Tom's Midnight Garden* by Philippa Pearce

I was a hungry reader as a child. I took books out from the local library each week, losing myself eagerly inside them. And I had a small collection of my own books – two shelves' worth above my bed, mostly Christmas and birthday presents – which I read over and over. A child's reading is very different to an adult's. An adult begins each book critically: suspiciously, even. Is this writing any good, has the writer got anything to say? A child takes on trust whatever book is in her hands – filling out its thinness, if it is thin, with her own imagination. And yet, perhaps discrimination was going on at some level, even in my childhood. There were a few beloved books – fiction always, first and last – that were at the core of my reading, revisited over and over, forming my imagination and the shape of my world.

One of these favourites, Philippa Pearce's *Tom's Midnight Garden*, appears to me now like a bridge between my childhood and my adult taste in reading. When I revisit its opening pages, I'm struck by the quality of the writing – the complex ideas and elegant sentences, the vivid detail. Tom has been sent to stay with his uncle and aunt at the beginning of the summer holidays because his brother has measles; he's resentful and hostile. The tone is grave, taking what the boy feels and sees with a whole seriousness – no bouncing, jolly condescension to the child reader. Yet there's an implicit criticism, too, of Tom's impatient judgement of his kindly aunt and tetchy uncle. No doubt the gravity of the prose, along with the psychological complexity, were part of what attracted me. Above all, though, I loved the brilliant conceit at the heart of the story, which was in tune with so much of my own curiosity and anxiety as a child.

Uncle Alan and Aunt Gwen live in a rented flat in a large house; the old lady who owns the whole house, Mrs Bartholomew, lives on the top floor. Once this house had a great garden, but it's built over now and only a dingy small yard is left, with dustbins in it and a garage. Poor angry Tom, bored and wakeful, creeps downstairs into the hall one night when his aunt and uncle are asleep, to find out why the grandfather clock strikes 13 instead of midnight. When he opens the back door, which ought to lead into the yard, he finds in its place a magnificent garden with lawns and flowerbeds, great yew trees and glasshouses. The garden is only there at night when the clock strikes; by day there's just the dreary yard with its dustbins.

Night after night, Tom spends long happy hours in the garden. He meets a girl in there, Hatty, and the two lonely children become friends: there's something very adult and truthful in the way Philippa Pearce writes their uneasy, wary, tender relationship. And yet, when Tom gets back to his bed in the flat, it's only ever a few minutes after midnight. In his daytime life, the days pass slowly enough – but time in the garden moves differently, the seasons come and go, Hatty changes and begins to seem like a young woman. One night, Tom and Hatty leave the garden and go skating on the frozen river – it's a culmination and it's also the moment he knows she's slipping away from him. It turns out eventually – of course, of course, but the first time I hadn't seen it coming! – that young Hatty in the garden in the past of the house is the same person as old Mrs Bartholomew in its present.

This twist of plot unlocked so much for me, it haunted and obsessed me. I had always been haunted, as soon as I could think, by the idea of time. The past had been the present once. This present, which was fitted so tightly around me, and seemed so irrefutably real for as long as it lasted – where did it go? 'Tom was thinking about the Past, that Time made so far away. Time had taken this Present of Hatty's and turned it into his Past.' The old people I knew, my grandparents and their friends, must have been children once. The rooms of the houses I knew had been lived in once by other people, been furnished with their furniture, been the scene of their pleasures and their dramas.

I am still haunted and obsessed by the same things. The kind of fiction I write tries to capture the arrangements and style and sensations of a particular present, tries to find a language for how we live *right now*, in this place, in this historical moment. And as that moment passes and is left behind, the best books and films and paintings continue to hold its shape. Rereading *Tom's Midnight Garden* now, I can almost reach out and touch my child self, who loved this book more than half a century ago. And I'm touching, too, that lost world of the 1950s, Tom's present, when the book was written, and beyond that a late Victorian world when the midnight garden thrived and Hatty was a child. Hatty's Victorian world was still close enough, in the 1950s, to be within living memory; but it's slipping away from us now and becoming the deep, lost past, only kept alive for us in art.

Tessa Hadley is the British author of eight novels, including The Past, Late in The Day *and* Free Love, *and three short story collections. She has contributed short stories to the* New Yorker *for 20 years.*

George the Poet

on *Outliers* by Malcolm Gladwell

I first read *Outliers* when I was 21. I'd been studying sociology for about five years and was deep into figuring out society and my environment. Why was it that the deeper I got into education, the more distant I became from my childhood friends? Why did personal success feel like it was taking me further away from my community? That's when I found Malcolm Gladwell.

The book's fundamental premise is that success doesn't happen in isolation. It's a combination of people and chance that leads to any successful moment or successful outcome for a group of people. It allowed me to see that the chances that I was given in life that set me apart from my community early on were set in place by big events and long chains of consequence. *Outliers* led to a fundamental shift in my thinking. I no longer looked at success as a question of effort and genius alone, but as a series of connections.

In *Outliers*, Gladwell talks about communities and people who have exceptional outcomes in something, like Bill Gates and Steve Jobs. Clearly, he says, these people are exceptional in some respect. But let's also take a look at what's staring us in the face. These men were both born in the same year. They were both 21 years old with just enough independence and economic freedom to take advantage of the computer revolution at the same time. They had access to computers before the general population. There's this constant pulling of that thread in his work.

To illustrate his point about the collective advantage, he talks about a community based in Philadelphia who are originally from Sicily and have a much higher life expectancy and quality of life than the rest of the state. He says it's because they have inherited traditions from their homelands and keep their lives very simple. They value social connections. They eat the same food their ancestors ate hundreds of years ago. They are supportive of each other as a community.

Gladwell is a skilled and talented storyteller who uses true case studies – some big historical stuff, some small personal stuff – to weave a narrative. It really influenced me growing up. In my work, whether it's rap or spoken poetry, the stories I tell are either based on real events or they are looking to make a serious point. Like Gladwell, I am overtly sociological and intentionally academic in my work. I organise my stories academically so as to kill two birds with one stone: talk to young people and help them learn. I believe that difficult stuff should be made accessible. If the maximum number of people are not involved in a necessary conversation simply because you need a Ph.D. to discuss it, that's not fair. We are living this stuff. We are part of this stuff. We should be able to get that from the art that we enjoy the most.

I read *Outliers* as a book and I also listened to the audiobook, which is read by the author. Listening to Malcolm Gladwell read by Malcolm Gladwell allows me to experience his words in my body differently to how I experience the written word. With the written word, I am the filter. When I read it, I want to put the George voice on it. But if I can hear it from the author's mouth, there's a transfer of energy. It sounds a little bit hippy and flowery, but if you consider that sound is vibrational energy that lands in your ear, and that the reaction of that vibration in your body is unique to your body, then it's literally and scientifically a transfer of energy.

I would recommend *Outliers* to anyone who is unsure of their place in the world. Life can be very scary when you try to find purpose in an isolated existence. But when you look around you, and you think about how others impact you, and how you impact others, some things become self-evident. The context of your life is your community. We all affect each other, and we cannot ignore that by isolating people's actions. Art can provide a space where we are able to see this. It feels like Gladwell is trying to hold up a mirror: how we treat each other, how valuable our time and space is, when we share it. And, like me, he is using the academic and creative space to do so.

George Mpanga, best known by his stage name George the Poet, is a British-Ugandan rapper and spoken-word poet. He is best-known for his BBC podcast, Have You Heard George's Podcast?*, which blends memoir, reportage and social politics and has won multiple British Podcast Awards and a Peabody Award.*

Marian Keyes

on *Cold Comfort Farm* by Stella Gibbons

It was 1990, and I had gone away by myself to
Santorini for two weeks. I was so disappointed
in my life at that point – suicidal and drinking
alcoholically – and I hoped that if I flung myself
into a location far away, wonderful things would
happen. Anyone who goes to a Greek island
on their own for two weeks will *surely* have an
adventure, I thought. But I didn't, and I was
incredibly lonely. It was long before mobile phones
and social media. My saving grace was that before
I'd left, I'd asked three women I worked with at
the Architectural Association in Bloomsbury to
lend me books that they loved. I didn't question
what they brought in; I just took them all.

I remember there was some Nancy Mitford in
there, a Barbara Vine and also *Cold Comfort Farm*
by Stella Gibbons. I was baffled by it initially. It's
a satire of those 'loam and lovechild' books where
everyone is miserable and inbred and fecund,

and I wasn't familiar with books that satirised. At that point, I read in just two categories. Mid-century American white men, like Joseph Heller, Truman Capote, Ernest Hemingway, that muscular confident statement-y kind of writing, because my dad belonged to a book club and got sent books like this. And then on the other hand there were the books that I *really* loved: Jilly Cooper, Judith Krantz. But *Cold Comfort Farm* didn't fit into either category. It was subversive and unexpected, elegant and cold. I normally really don't like cold writers, but then I clicked that underneath the coldness was this twinkle and it just grabbed me.

Cold Comfort Farm was written in 1932 but set in a semi-mythical future of 1949, where Mayfair has become a slum. (Just imagine.) Flora Poste's parents have died, and she is left with only £100 a year to live on and so her great-aunt Ada takes her in at the very rural, completely falling apart *Cold Comfort Farm*. Everyone living there has these stunted ambitions and thwarted romances where everything is always going wrong until Flora storms in to organise their lives. It's both absurd and oddly believable. It's set in one of those communities where there is nothing to do but make your own entertainment and where people argue about absolutely nothing.

I loved it because it was funny in this very eccentric way and I love a bit of eccentricity, in both a person and a book. (I like it in my own writing, too.) They wash the dishes with something called a clettering stick – which is what my husband and I call the scrubbing brush – and when she first moves to Cold Comfort Farm, Flora hears her cousin talking about stealing feathers from the hens to trim dolls' hats. It was just the funniest thing I'd ever read. The humour really, really lifted me during this very dark time. It's not a book about love or emotional growth – not like *Heartburn* by Nora Ephron, which is another of my favourite books and by a real pal. But *Cold Comfort Farm* showed me how you can construct an unexpected reality to produce something unexpected and hugely entertaining. I will also reluctantly admit that I am quite like Flora Poste. I am the organiser in my family and they are always joking about me with the clipboard. Someone has to be the organiser, I say! Nothing would happen otherwise. But it's also true that I don't like not having the power. I like people to arrive on time and things to happen when they are meant to happen or I get quite jittery.

When I got back to London, I spoke to a couple of the learned older women who had lent me the books. They told me that there was a sequel to *Cold Comfort Farm*, but that I shouldn't read it. And so, I never did. I didn't have much money at the time so I figured if no one was going to lend it to me, I wasn't going to buy it. But I'm not intrigued by the sequel. I feel like this one's quite enough. I reread it about every five years or so.

I had no idea when I first read it that I wanted to write. It wasn't until I was 30, when my life had totally begun to shut down, that I wrote *Watermelon*. And when I came to write, I thought of this book, and how you have to intrigue people, how you have to pull the rug from under their feet, and how you have to be funny. There are no layers of bullshit to *Cold Comfort Farm*, and what that taught me is that I don't care about genre or writing style; the only thing that matters to me is authenticity. This thing of 'persevering' with a book – why in the name of God would you persevere? Reading is meant to be a pleasure, an escape from the shittiness and the rest of it. I will only read something that I love. And I will only write something that I love. And the best bit is that that only gets easier as you get older.

Marian Keyes is the Irish author of 15 novels, including Rachel's Holiday, Grown Ups *and* Sushi for Beginners, *and two collections of journalism. One of the most successful Irish novelists of all time, she has sold over 40 million books globally and was named the Author of the Year at the 2022 British Book Awards.*

Elif Shafak

on *Orlando* by Virginia Woolf

I was an avid reader and writer from an early age, mostly because I was an only child. I lived in Ankara with my grandmother in a very conservative and inward-looking neighbourhood, and my mother and I were outsiders. I was born in France, and after my parents separated, my mother brought me back to Turkey. She was a young divorcee with no career. Usually, women in such situations would immediately marry again. A young divorcee is considered a threat. Neighbours would suggest suitable husbands to her. But my grandmother intervened and said that she would raise me so that my mother could go back to university. 'If she wants to get married, she can, but then it will be a choice,' she said.

My grandmother had been denied a proper education and she whole heartedly believed in women's education. Her support and solidarity changed our lives. My mum went back to university, learned six languages and entered the foreign ministry. Thanks to that, we travelled and I had a good education. And all of that was possible because of that critical moment in time. It instilled in me an understanding of the importance of solidarity between women.

Not many people read in Turkey, because reading is not really encouraged – especially not novels, let alone novels by women. Books are not necessarily banned, but the authors are demonised, incarcerated, exiled or prosecuted. Anything you write can offend the authorities and you can be put on trial. It's also a feminist issue. More than 75 per cent of illiterate people in Turkey are women. But those that do read, do so passionately. And I was one of them. I was deep into my Russian male literature phase when I first read *Orlando*. I was 18, and even though I didn't understand all of it on first reading, I felt very much connected to the book and to Woolf.

Orlando is a courageous book, full of chutzpah. It was published in 1928 and on the front cover it says that it's a biography. The book is not a biography, of course. Woolf is challenging us, blurring the boundaries right from the very start. The book describes the journey of an aristocratic poet who travels across genders, geography and time meeting key figures of literary and cultural history. In order to understand *Orlando*, we also need to understand the big love affair Woolf had with fellow author Vita Sackville-West. I am bisexual, and I hadn't seen at that point any books questioning gender norms and a more fluid identity. Woolf felt like a kindred spirit, and I felt very much connected.

Another incredibly important detail – more than a detail, in fact – is that Orlando changes sex in Turkey. Constantinople (now Istanbul) was a very cosmopolitan and fluid place throughout its complex history with no fixed identity. It feels so sad to me that if this book was written by a Turkish writer, it would most probably be attacked, censured or even prosecuted in my motherland. Turkey has a long and rich history, but that doesn't translate into a strong memory. Society has a collective amnesia. Our entire relationship is full of ruptures. That void is filled in by an ultra-nationalist perception of the past. In that reading of history, you don't speak about pluralism. What was history like for women? What was history like for minorities? Those questions are never asked, so their stories become untold stories and taboos. If you talk about them, you are labelled a betrayer. Virginia Woolf saw the importance of that diverse nature of Constantinople and appreciated it. But many Turkish people have never been allowed to acknowledge it.

In *A Room of One's Own*, there's an interesting argument that Woolf explored. It is called 'Shakespeare's sister', where she asks if Shakespeare had had a sister and she had exactly the same talents, what would her life be like? Would she be given the same opportunities? She would have gone crazy or shot herself or ended up very lonely. Women, after all, could not live a free life and write in the Elizabethan era. In 2007, I wrote a half-memoir called *Black Milk* where I took Woolf's essay and applied it to a famous 16th-century Turkish poet called Fuzuli. What if Fuzuli had had a sister called Firuze, I asked – what would her life be like? The truth is that she would never be allowed to publish her work. Even if she wrote, she would be consigned to oblivion, because she was a woman.

I associate *Orlando* with freedom. Virginia Woolf is an amazing writer, but she is also a public intellectual and a thinker. That side is not emphasised enough. She is also fiercely feminist. Feminism is vilified in Turkey. It is considered a Western import. In literature we have the tradition of the flâneur. He strolls around the city and he's always male. In *Orlando*, we see the city through the female gaze. Putting women in the public space like this is the ultimate act of courage.

Elif Shafak is a Turkish-British novelist, essayist, activist and political scientist, whose books have been translated into over 50 languages. The most widely read female author in Turkey, she has written 12 novels and seven works of non-fiction. She is an honorary fellow at St Anne's College, Oxford, a Vice President of the Royal Society of Literature and has been awarded a Chevalier of the Order of Arts and Letters.

Derek Owusu

on *The Great Gatsby* by F. Scott Fitzgerald

The first time I read *The Great Gatsby*, I was at work, sitting at the reception of a sports centre at Bolton University. I was about 25, a late uni goer, and had taken it out of the library. Or so I thought. The book I took out said *The Great Gatsby*, had a glistening silver finish on the cover, and I remember I felt so excited that I'd finally be able to read the book my best friend had been raving about for over a year. I wasn't much of a reader at the time, and she was trying to get me to read the classics, whatever they were. But when I got to work and started reading, I wondered why the introduction was taking so long. Turns out, I had taken out an analysis of *The Great Gatsby* and not the actual novel.

I took my break early and checked out the real thing. I finished it the same day in my dorm room and didn't feel much, mostly because I didn't really understand it. The language was complicated to a novice like me, but I was determined to decipher the mystery of Gatsby and the flowery prose of Nick Carraway. I began reading it again immediately.

On the second reading, I felt like I was reading a completely different book. Sentences moved me enough to put the book down, spreading the centre of the page I was on, rub my arms to feel the piloerection, take a deep breath and say, wow. This was the most beautiful thing I had ever seen. I saw the book as a whole; even though I was reading page after page, there was something complete about it as I followed each perfectly chosen word and mysterious narrative. I understood everything and knew Gatsby was someone like ... me.

And that's strange to most people because we couldn't be more different objectively. But it's a hallmark of great literature. To me. Gatsby was working class, struggling to find his identity, thinking love would make him who he always wanted to be, thinking money could change the circumstances of his birth and relying on myth to elevate him in the world. He courted friends but preferred to be alone, thinking only of how he was perceived and caring nothing about being received. Except for one person. And she was arguably the jewel to complete the accumulating gold to aid his ascension. He couldn't accept himself so others doing it for him was the next best thing. He even had a 'tag name' as so many from working-class backgrounds do: Gatsby.

The Great Gatsby taught me what I love most about literature – the writing, the ability to put sentences together in a way to evoke feelings you'll never have words for, and that's okay, just to let the impression and music of the language marinate and make you feel: excited, impressed, sad, jealous. It taught me about ideas that convey humanity, that even if a character isn't traditionally three-dimensional, everything they're missing or omitting makes them human in the imagination and acts as a guide to seeing particular life circumstances as they are.

And this is what I aspire to do in my writing. I want to create impressions for the reader rather than impress them with the plot. The plot of *The Great Gatsby* is a simple and straightforward one, but how it is expressed has a lasting impact. This is a book I recommend to everyone. Though I admit it's not to everyone's taste. Either because they studied it in school or they find the prose too purple or the narrative boring. But I feel it will always be relevant in a world that forces us to constantly aspire, to achieve more and amass our riches by any means possible.

Gatsby meant so much to me, I even had his name tattooed on my shoulder like an obsessed lover, but it's because the novel isn't about the characters, it's about the prevailing and everlasting emotion of wanting more in a life that can promise us nothing but love, whether we have riches or not. We Gatsbys, we'll always turn out all right in the end. Life may remain static; but hope can carry us forward.

Derek Owusu is a British-Ghanaian writer, poet and podcaster, whose 2020 debut novel, That Reminds Me, *won the Desmond Elliott prize. The former host of literary podcast* Mostly Lit, *he also edited a 2019 anthology,* Safe: On Black British Men Reclaiming Space.

Ali Smith

on *The Summer Book* by Tove Jansson

The Summer Book is one of 10 books the Finnish writer and illustrator Tove Jansson wrote 'for adults'. It's one of my favourite books. Other Jansson favourites of mine are her brilliant books 'for children' about the Moomin family, an open and inclusive family of creatures curious and philosophical about everything, who survive wild climates and even wilder plotlines in the mountains and forests of Scandinavia, and she's world famous for these. But I've used quote marks in those two sentences because the distinctions between adult books and children's books blow away to nothing whenever you read Jansson, because at any age, reading these books, and especially this book, becomes a gift of understanding of all our ages in us at once.

The Summer Book is about an old woman and her small grandchild spending a summer on a very small island. 'It was just the same long summer always, and everything lived and grew at its own pace.' They talk and they fight and they go on adventures. There are dangers and darknesses: the child's mother is dead, but the death is mentioned in a dream image only, suitcases floating away in the water round the island. And is that water too deep for a child who can't yet swim very well? And why on earth has the person on the neighbouring island locked the doors of his house when everyone always leaves their doors open on these islands?

Age means experience, yes? Youth means everything new. But *The Summer Book* is a book of profound openness, where age knows everything anew and youth is profound experience. Saying this, or trying to describe the book in any way at all, doesn't come anywhere near what happens when you read it: the calm, the joy, the depth, the understanding, the warmth of this slim little masterpiece about everything.

The lightness of its writing, day or night, dark or light, is a kind of magic.

Ali Smith is a Scottish writer and playwright. The author of 11 novels and four short story collections, she has been nominated for the Booker Prize multiple times, and has won the Women's Prize for Fiction, the Goldsmiths Prize and the *Orwell Prize for Political Fiction. She has also written numerous plays. She is an honorary fellow at Goldsmiths and the University of East Anglia.*

Paris Lees

on *The Beach* by Alex Garland

I remember being bemused when our GCSE English teacher told us that people had felt strong physical reactions to books like *Frankenstein*, *Dracula* and other Gothic fiction when they first came out. To me, and the rest of the class, this seemed unlikely. We were raised on a diet of endless cable channels, mobile phones and video games. Constant stimulation. The idea that people had fainted while reading a book – perhaps even felt a sexual twinge mingled in with the anxiety – seemed ridiculous. So, I quietly filed it under 'things about the past I don't get', like how people didn't die of boredom before TV was invented. Until I read *The Beach*, that is.

I was 19 when I first picked up a copy of Alex Garland's cult 1996 novel. I'd been to see the film a few years earlier. It was a 15, and I wasn't, but me and my best friend managed to sneak in, keen to see Leonardo DiCaprio prancing around topless for two hours, his first movie after *Titanic*. I'd recently moved to a beach myself. Not the paradise described in *The Beach*, sadly, but Brighton seafront. I was the first person in my family to go to university and was desperate for adventure, excitement and to become well-read. I'd always loved books and I consumed them ravenously, often walking down the street with one in my hand. Such was life before Instagram.

The Beach is cool. Cooler than the film. The fact it had come out over 10 years previously by the time I read it only made it cooler to me. As a child in the 1990s, I felt like all the young adults around me were having fun. Rave culture was mainstream, particularly on the council estate I grew up on, and I had a young mum. Alex Garland was 26 when *The Beach* was published, and my mum was around the same age. I remember her going out clubbing and listening to The Prodigy, and how exciting it all seemed. It's this energy that Garland perfectly taps into. As the *Guardian* puts it, *The Beach* 'captured the late-90s zeitgeist'.

But it's the book's creeping, overwhelming sense of dread that made the biggest impression on me. Without giving any spoilers away, there's a moment where the narrator, Richard, gets himself into a suffocating situation. It's genuinely terrifying and I was so engrossed in the story, I felt as though I were right there with him. My heart was pounding. I was, like contemporary readers of Gothic fiction, having a strong physical and emotional reaction. Possibly even a twinge.

Plot and character matter, but it's the vivid scenes in *The Beach* that have stayed with me. It lives in me like a remembered nightmare or fever dream: it's a place I feel I've been to in my mind. Like all great works of art, it helps furnish my inner world. I reread it when I was 25 and still loved it, but it had lost a smidgen of its thrill. I'm grateful, now, that I read it as a teenager, when I was at my most impulsive and wild. It's dark and fun, a book to read when you're discovering life and hormones make the world exciting and intense.

I love how *The Beach* is peppered with references to cartoons, Nintendo and the Vietnam War. It feels so specific and lively. When I came to write my first book, *What It Feels Like for a Girl*, I wanted to create a sort of culture-soup, sprinkled with adverts, songs and slang that no one had thought about for years.

And while I wouldn't compare my writing to Garland per se, I'm definitely influenced by writers who make the reader feel something. I want a book to make me cry. Laugh. Angry. Disgusted. Horrified. I read to escape, to live for a while in the world that's created on the page, but I also want to feel something. Anything. That connection is the biggest joy a reader can experience and the highest compliment a writer can receive. Forget reviews. Just tell me you cried. Tell me you had to put the book down because it was too much. Tell me you remember how it made you feel 20 years later. As Maya Angelou puts it, 'People won't remember what you said, but they will remember how you made them feel.' The details of *The Beach* have become blurry, but I'll never forget the fear, the excitement and the beating of my heart.

Paris Lees is a British journalist and the author of a work of autofiction, What It Feels Like for a Girl. *The first openly trans columnist for British* Vogue, *and the first trans presenter for Radio 1, Channel 4 and guest on BBC 1's* Question Time, *she has also received an honorary doctorate from Brighton University.*

Dolly Alderton

on *Heartburn* by Nora Ephron

There are three things that are impossible to write. Food, flirting and heartbreak. We all eat, we've all lusted, we've all lost someone we love. And yet putting these experiences on the page in a way that is real and original, without leaning on cliché or sentimentality, is quite the task. God, I've tried. I've spent hours in front of a blank screen and a blinking cursor, wrestling with metaphors to conjure taste, dialogue to create chemistry and descriptions of unrequited love that don't sound like the lyrics to a Gary Barlow song. *Heartburn* by Nora Ephron, the most-loved and most-read book on my shelf, effortlessly nails all three. It is the study of a whole relationship in 150 or so pages – a marriage's architecture, rupture and its eventual demolition.

The narrator Rachel, a food writer, tells us what it was like to fall in love with her husband Mark, including an unbelievably sexy passage in which he teaches her how to dance: 'Your waist is mine for the next three minutes,' he tells her. 'After that I'll give it back. But you have to give it to me for now.' She describes the lustful stupor they fall into: 'We went out to dinner. And then we went to bed. We stayed there for about three weeks.' Followed by domestic, carb-filled bliss: 'Whenever I fall in love, I begin with potatoes. Sometimes meat and potatoes and sometimes fish and potatoes, but always potatoes. I have made a lot of mistakes falling in love, and regretted most of them, but never the potatoes that went with them.' And then, for the majority of the book, she describes heartbreak. Or, as she physically experiences it, heartburn, while she tries to make sense of his infidelity, which she discovers when seven months pregnant with their second baby.

Sounds miserable, doesn't it? When described like that, it seems bizarre that such a dark story (based on real-life events) became the plot of such a treasured book. But while it is raw and painful in moments, *Heartburn* is also hilarious. It is a unique portrait of heartbreak because Ephron finds the unexpected details of emotional devastation – the absurdity, mundanity and embarrassment of it. One of my favourite sections is when Rachel takes her son, leaves the marital home and goes to stay with her dad. The following morning, she hears the doorbell and assumes it is her husband Mark begging for her forgiveness. But instead, it is Jonathan, the husband of the woman with whom Mark is having an affair. They burst into tears and fall into each other's arms. 'Oh Jonathan, isn't it awful?' Rachel says. Jonathan replies: 'What's happening to this country?', before Rachel explains to us in an aside: 'Jonathan never takes anything personally; he always sees himself as a statistical reflection of a larger trend in society.'

I've often wondered if the reason *Heartburn* is so exquisitely put together is because it is the confluence of all of Ephron's jobs. She was a newspaper reporter, a screenwriter and a personal essayist. All these particular skills layer up in the storytelling as deliciously as the Potatoes Anna recipe Rachel gives us (layers of potato slices and butter. The basis of every Ephron recipe is butter). Her journalistic training is channelled through her highly observant narrator. Her skills as a moviemaker make for perfect scenes of dialogue (the chapter in which her therapy group is robbed at gunpoint is a particular highlight; all of them fighting over whose fault it was and who should get the limelight). And her ability to open up her heart and let her readers in feels intimate and precious. Nora, through Rachel, speaks directly to you. It is unfathomable to me that this is so many people's favourite book, because every time I read it, I truly believe it was written just for me.

The book is often called a thinly disguised novel. Like Rachel's husband, Nora Ephron's husband, the journalist Carl Bernstein, had an affair while Nora was pregnant with their second child. Their breakup was very public. Nora's infamous mantra, borrowed from her writer mother, is that 'everything is copy', so it is unsurprising that such a life event should end up in her work. But it is still a piece of work rather than a piece of therapy, and to reduce this beautiful novel to a large tell-all confession is to grossly undermine it.

Fiction is memoir and memoir is fiction. Writers use reality to enrich our make-believe, and we shape and reorder the real events of our lives when we're writing it into a piece of non-fiction. In an introduction to a later edition of the book, Ephron wrote: 'One of the things I'm proudest of is that I managed to convert an event that seemed so hideously tragic at the time to a comedy – and if that's not fiction, I don't know what is.' I don't care about what's real and what isn't in *Heartburn*. Any traces of Bernstein and Ephron hidden in the sentences is the least important thing about the book. The thing everyone loves about it is its humour and its emotional truth. It will always make me laugh; it will always make me cry. And of all the things I've ever tried, it remains the most effective medication for a broken heart.

Dolly Alderton is a British journalist, novelist, screenwriter and podcaster, best known for her 2018 memoir, Everything I Know About Love, *which won a National Book Award and which she adapted for TV for the BBC. A columnist for the* Sunday Times Style *magazine and the former co-host of* The High Low *podcast, she is also the author of a novel,* Ghosts.

Paul Mendez

on *Escape to An Autumn Pavement* by Andrew Salkey

I first encountered the Jamaican novelist and poet Andrew Salkey in Somerset House's 2018 *Get Up, Stand Up!* exhibition. On display was *The Lime* (1974), a group portrait by the Trinidadian filmmaker Horace Ové, in which Salkey and *The Lonely Londoners* author Sam Selvon flank John La Rose, the co-founder of New Beacon Books. Almost incognito under a deep bucket hat, horn-rimmed glasses and a wild beard, and with his fists jammed in his raincoat pockets, he looks every bit the writer's writer, appreciated by those in the know and content to be largely ignored by the unliterary masses. The Windrush generation produced a rich seam of literature, thanks much to Salkey's work behind the scenes, from his presenting of the BBC's *Caribbean Voices* to his own poetry, children's fiction and retellings of Anancy folk tales and from his prominent early roles in V. S. Naipaul's career to the founding of the Caribbean Artists' Movement.

Also on display in *Get Up, Stand Up!* was Ové's film *Baldwin's Nigger* (1969), documenting James Baldwin's seminal Q&A with a group of radical Black British students. Watching it again recently, I recognised the figure two seats away from Baldwin as Salkey and was delighted to see the two of them in such close proximity at the height of their powers, facing an electrified audience in a cramped room. After reading about Salkey's *Escape to an Autumn Pavement* in *The Cambridge History of Black and Asian British Writing*, which I reviewed (disastrously) for *The Times Literary Supplement*, I read *Escape to an Autumn Pavement* for the first time in May 2021, as lockdown restrictions were being incrementally eased.

It had been a year since my debut novel *Rainbow Milk* was published during the very first lockdown, and my entire professional life up to that point had taken place on Zoom and via email. My maternal grandmother, a true matriarch, died in October 2019, leaving me uncertain as to my position within the extended family, as she was the member I was closest to. Never had I gained so much only to feel such a loss, such a feeling of exile. My grandparents, who were of

Jamaican heritage, were always circumspect and conveniently forgetful about their lives during the Windrush era, yet lived in houses stacked with flowery wallpaper, loud carpets and cheap ornaments from the 1960s and 70s. Looking to enhance my sense of history with social realist Caribbean-British fiction, music and art, *Escape to an Autumn Pavement* stood out to me for the fact that it is one of the earliest examples of queer Black British writing, queerness often being seen as incompatible with what it means to be Black and part of a family.

The novel's plot, as far as there is one, forms naturally from the intersections of race, gender, colour, class, migration status, education and sexuality its hero carries around with him. Johnnie Sobert is an educated young Jamaican who has moved, like so many others, to the Mother Country, where he has to settle for jobs that are beneath him and for a place lower in the class system than he feels his education and light skin tone deserve. He lives in a boarding house in Hampstead and works in an underground Soho bar redolent of The Colony Club, a place of tolerance where the demi-monde mix with drunken aristocrats. Salkey's handling of Johnnie's bisexuality, as he is pursued by two of his housemates – one male, one (married) female – is strikingly devoid of judgement, drama or shame (especially for its time, pre-partial decriminalisation and as the author was presumed straight). The author's magnanimity emphasises Johnnie's ennui in postwar London, where lingering American GIs and tactless members of the public racially profile him, while his masculinity is questioned by women put out by his lack of interest in them. At a Black barbershop, Johnnie is open about his predicament and receives a response that confirms his suspicion that he is too Black to be English and too English (and queer) to be Black.

I sometimes think about my GCSE syllabus, and the novels, plays and poetry I was set, that virtually exclusively promoted white, heterosexual, patriarchal points of view, and now understand why, for a long time, I read sparsely: I was not able to examine or reconcile my Black and queer subjectivities in those narratives. I believe that, had I been given authors like Salkey, Baldwin and Edgar Mittelholzer (the Guyanese writer whose 1950 novel *A Morning at the Office* is among the very first in Black British fiction to feature a gay character) to study, I would've taken myself seriously as a writer earlier. Better late than never, though, and while I acknowledge *Escape* contains some stereotypical depictions of characters that will appear dated to us, I'm inspired by Salkey's emotional prose, cutting dialogue and essayistic musings.

Escape to an Autumn Pavement was greeted with critical silence on original release, most unfairly given Salkey's enthusiastic promotion of other authors, but as someone who is trying to reclaim my heritage as a Black, gay man and descendant of Jamaican immigrants, I declare it canonical.

Paul Mendez is the Jamaican-British author of Rainbow Milk, *which was shortlisted for a British Book Award and the Jhalak Prize. He is currently adapting the novel for TV and studying for an MA in Black British Literature at Goldsmiths, University of London.*

Jojo Moyes

on *National Velvet* by Enid Bagnold

I was quite an eccentric child. I had an enormous imagination and I read all the time as I was an only child with no television. I was also totally and utterly horse-obsessed, writing long tedious stories about girls and their ponies in my lined exercise books. I once asked my mother to fill my bedroom with hay so that I could pretend to be a horse and she agreed, which was particularly amazing of her considering we lived in Hackney. Neither of my parents are remotely horsey, they are in the arts, and they got this weird kid who wanted to sniff pony ears.

I have read *National Velvet* by Enid Bagnold so many times that I couldn't even tell you when I first read it – but I'm going to estimate that I was nine. A lot of people are only familiar with *National Velvet* because of Elizabeth Taylor. But the original non-Hollywood version is so much more nuanced and interesting. It's about a normal, quite eccentric family who win a horse in a raffle that goes on to win the Grand National. It was published in 1935, but it feels very modern. The characters come alive, because they are quirky and unsentimental and you would recognise the dynamics of the family that she wrote in a family today.

It has at its heart this little girl with digestive problems who achieves something impossible through sheer force of will. I was a very weedy child, always the tiniest person in the class. I was like a country child, born in a city. I wanted to be with animals and horses and so this became an emblematic book for me. It was about somebody I understood – who was dreamy and solitary and sickly but steely when it came to pursuing something.

I had no writers in my family. There was a man at the end of my road called Sheldon who had written a book on voodoo and he was the most writerly person I knew. I associated writers with thick black glasses in garrets in Paris. It was only after 10 years in journalism that I thought I might have a voice. I'd had a baby and realised you can't be a news reporter and have a small baby unless something gives – and I didn't want it to be the baby. Also, *Bridget Jones* had come out and it was like this total revelation in publishing.

I was working at the *Independent* newspaper where Bridget Jones was first a column and I found myself in that initial explosion of 'chick lit'. It was very female, often quite funny, often tackling quite tough issues but ultimately in a very readable way.

I kept reading these books and thinking, 'I could do that'. It took me three books to get published. Looking back, I can only think it is that same bloody-mindedness that Velvet Brown, the little girl, has in the book that led me to carry on. I couldn't not write, just like she couldn't not ride a horse. I wrote eight books before *Me Before You* came out. When I read those unpublished books back – they're all longhand on paper – I think, 'I wasn't good enough.' I had to learn how to do it, and it had to come from bitter experience.

While my fates were changing, I kept on going back and reading *National Velvet*. I got something different out of it every time I read it. When I was young, I very much identified with Velvet. And now when I read it, I identify with her mother. What I love about Ma Brown is that whilst her relationship with Velvet is adoring and facilitating, it's not remotely sentimental. Ma Brown is one of life's stoics. 'No use guessing and dreading,' she says to Velvet. Velvet sees her mother as elemental: she is a mountain or tree. She is grounded, she takes no nonsense and there is the loveliest meet-cute between her and the horse. Velvet's mother is walking down to the village, and as she is walking, she is thinking about her daughter's prospects. She thinks, who will be a suitor for Velvet? This odd child, who is dreamy and plays with paper horses. Suddenly, this horse comes clattering down the road and stops dead in front of Ma Brown and lowers its head, and Ma Brown says: 'A suitor for Velvet.' The mother can see what her child needs.

I couldn't even tell you who this book is aimed at. But I think great literature transcends age brackets. I'm a picky reader and I get something out of it every time I read it. You could read it aged eight to 80. An adult will pick up on the nuances that a child will not – about your dreams. That comes with sacrificing who you were to adulthood, and how germs of that can remain inside you.

Jojo Moyes is a British novelist and screenwriter, best known for her 2012 novel, Me Before You, *which sold 14 million copies worldwide and was adapted into a feature film starring Sam Claflin and Emilia Clarke. The author of 15 novels, she has sold over 38 million books worldwide.*

Diana Evans

on *Middlesex* by Jeffrey Eugenides

I read *Middlesex* by American novelist Jeffrey
Eugenides on a beach in Ko Samui, Thailand.
Sometimes I was in a hammock between two trees
with the ocean at the edge of my vision. Sometimes
the sea was behind me and I was lying on a mat
on the sand, completely enraptured. The book
went with me back to my yoga shack when the
sun went down. I took it with me to pranayama
sessions and left it at the edge of the hall in case
there was a minute to read. I read it on the bus
into town, on the plane, in the airport lounges.
I almost missed Thailand because of it. When
I think of Thailand, I also think of *Middlesex*, of
Detroit, of Greece and Mount Olympus.

The timing is significant. I had recently arrived at
a place of temporary freedom. I had been writing a
book, my first novel, for some years, a difficult novel,
one that I had doubted at several abandonments
along the way that I could ever finish. Eventually

I had taken it with me to do a creative writing MA in Norwich and there completed it, and soon afterwards got a publishing deal. That was how I was free. I was out of the other side of the long *26a* tunnel and had a little money to be a writer on a yoga retreat, plus I did not yet have children. I was in the before-time, at the threshold of the next projects of work and life, and my mind was gaping open for a good story. I fell in headlong.

It is of course the Pulitzer Prize-winning tale of Calliope Stephanides, who becomes Cal Stephanides, an intersex man born into a Greek-American family with a variant gene. The novel follows this gene all the way from its instigation in Asia Minor to its physical and psychic manifestation in its prime carrier, through his childhood in Detroit, his escape to San Francisco to discover his identity, and a portion of his adult life in Berlin from where he is narrating the story, drawing on some elements of Eugenides's own life and family history. It's a vast novel comprising social commentary and historical detail and churning, infectious humour, and its greatest strength is its mastery of character. It is character that makes it so unforgettable.

Character is the root of fiction, the very core, though not necessarily the beginning. The seed of an idea can begin with a place or a theme or an object or even a plot, but at some point in the process of gestation all this is met with character, which makes it dance, or shine, or reverberate. The human factor is the thing. The muscle of the human mind and experience, witnessing a world. Character is where the particularities and specificities that language is so joyously capable of can take centre-stage: the way people think, their exact idiosyncratic thoughts, the way they walk and gesture, the way they communicate with one another. Character is the gift of dialogue where a writer can pull reams of bright fabrics out of a person's mouth. I used to be scared of dialogue when I first began to write. Now I can hardly stop them talking, and when I am not writing, they are still talking in my head.

In *Middlesex*, there is a character, Cal's brother, called Chapter Eleven, who has stayed with me just for his name. His grandfather is called Lefty, and Lefty's wife, Cal's grandmother, is the riveting Desdemona Stephanides. She is the greatest example of a living, breathing character I have yet read in a novel, so much so that I can still hear her voice, the pitch and tone of it, 18 years after first reading her. I remember most of all her shrieking reaction to Lefty's gambling away of all their savings, which deserves quoting here. It is all in capital letters: 'HOW WILL WE EAT! …

WHAT KIND OF HUSBAND ARE YOU TO DO THIS TO YOUR WIFE WHO COOKED AND CLEANED FOR YOU AND GAVE YOU CHILDREN AND NEVER COMPLAINED!' So it goes on, accompanied by her staggering around the kitchen, beating on her chest and ripping off parts of her dress.

I felt like I knew Desdemona personally through witnessing the story of her life and the extremity of her emotional world. I even named a kiss after her in my novel *Ordinary People* because it seemed she deserved such resurrection in another dimension. The miracle of writing is that we can meet other people on a page. We can almost touch them. We can certainly be brought to understand them through the fact that we feel with them. It is sensory and spiritual contact with humanity across material distance. This is why books to me are like friends. They're full of people you can be alone with.

Diana Evans is a British-Nigerian journalist and author of three novels, including 26a, *which won a British Book Award, and* Ordinary People, *which was shortlisted for the Women's Prize for Fiction and the Orwell Prize for Political Fiction. She is an associate lecturer in creative writing at Goldsmiths, University of London and a Fellow of the Royal Society of Literature.*

Sebastian Faulks

on *The Last Swim* by J. J. Smith

I think I was about nine and, as happens quite often at that age, was ill in bed with a chest infection.

The book came from a mobile lending library that occasionally came to our village and I'm going to have to be quite frank about this, but I can't remember what it was called. For the sake of this little piece, let's say it was called *The Last Swim* and it was by an author called J. J. Smith.

The only author of that name that I can now find is a keto dietitian in America. Perhaps in my fevered state I misread the initials. But I found that the story exerted a strange grip from the first page. A family had gone on holiday to the seaside in a remote village in Wales. This was the kind of thing families did in those days, before 'abroad' had been discovered as a destination. I could identify with one of the children, an impetuous boy called Jacob who walked in a funny way and never seemed to get anything right. Although the family seemed quite normal – Dad smoked a pipe and made bad jokes, Mum did most of the work – there was something not quite right about them.

You felt you knew them, but you didn't. None of them was quite like anyone you might have met, and this is what made them interesting. The sister was called Naomi and she was a vexing daughter, disappearing after tea on the beach to meet a local boy of about 18 years old with a spotted neckerchief (the illustrations were line drawings, one or two in colour). Mum expressed her doubts, but Dad seemed quite carefree about it as he loaded up another pipe and refilled his teacup from the thermos.

A few days later they found their pet dog, a Collie-Alsatian cross called Cinders, dead in a farm lane. It was said that she had been worrying the sheep and had been shot by a farmer, but Jacob for one wasn't sure about this and that evening went off to do some investigating. Behind a whitewashed pub with a black slate roof, he saw a field in which several young locals were making some sort of meeting place from hay bales.

When his parents were in bed that night, he crept out of the cottage and made his way to the field. Lit by torches, a young woman was standing in the middle of a group of people and seemed to be conducting some sort of ceremony. Jacob watched from behind a tree, and what struck him most of all was that the woman was naked. He seemed to find this upsetting, though in a strangely enjoyable way he didn't want to think about.

I suppose J. J. Smith had read a fair amount of Enid Blyton, but he had a darker and more violent streak. There was some smuggling going on, for sure, and I was familiar with this from countless Blyton stories, but it was a surprise to find the local postmistress, shy Miss Wilson, strangled behind the counter one morning. It was also worrying to see Naomi spending so much time with the untrustworthy local youths and their motorbikes. You could tell they were untrustworthy from the illustration.

As the story went on, and it cracked along pretty fast, we discovered new aspects of each character. Smith returned to each in turn after a few pages away and twisted them a few degrees in the light so that they revealed a different facet. Dad's bonhomie was a false front for a deep kind of melancholy caused by his experiences in a recent war. Mum had chosen this village for their holiday not because it was idyllic (it clearly wasn't) but because her lover was rumoured to live there.

Most strange of all was Jacob. I wasn't sure that I could still identify with him when he seemed drawn to the naked woman, yet he had a fire and independence of character that was thrilling. His physical courage when he crept out at night and witnessed the rituals or took photographs of the smugglers' hideout was impressive, especially when it was revealed about two-thirds of the way through the book that his odd way of walking was due to childhood polio.

The climax brought everything together: the mother's secret and the father's sadness; Naomi's wild longings and Jacob's impulsive bravery. Against the pressure of time, Jacob had to swim from the smugglers' island to the mainland against a running tide. Only if he made it in time would Naomi be saved from death by burning. The waves beat against him as he strove and kicked with his one good leg, lungs burning, the muscles in his shoulders 'begging for release'. It was not just the safety of the family and the triumph of Good that hung on his making it safely to the shore. The author had shown that all his characters were creatures of history and prisoners of their human limitations. All our lives depended on Jacob's last swim.

Fourteen years later, after I had discovered that the author was in fact a woman, I submitted my own first novel to a publisher under the pen name of J. J. Smith. I thought it seemed propitious.

Sadly (for me, though not for the reading public), it was rejected.

Sebastian Faulks is a British writer and broadcaster, best known for Birdsong, *which won the British Book of the Year in 1994, was adapted for both theatre and TV and has been named one of Britain's best-loved novels. The author of 15 novels and four works of non-fiction, he is a Fellow of the Royal Society of Literature and was awarded a CBE in 2002.*

Lisa Taddeo

on *Fever Dream* by Samanta Schweblin

The first time I got drunk after becoming a mother culminated with one of the worst hangovers of my life. My daughter was just about two. It was the first time we'd gotten a babysitter, and the occasion was my birthday. My husband did it all by himself: secured the babysitter, who inexplicably/predictably ate everything in our fridge, and made the impossible-to-get reservation at the hot new sushi spot. I was stratospherically impressed and excited. We ate copious amounts of sea urchin, and I drank my weakness, hot sake, like it was life-giving green tea.

The next morning was full of sun and my daughter was thrilled to be alive. I heard her bound into my room though I could not see her because my eyes were swollen shut with the mean glue of booze. I asked my husband for one more present. Please take our child away from me so she won't see her mother like this, like the college girl she once was, bent over the toilet, crying, hating herself for having those last four carafes of sake. If only she had stopped at three.

He took our daughter to the park, and I did something I hadn't had the luxury of doing during the day in such a long time – I read. I read an entire book. The book was called *Fever Dream* by Samanta Schweblin and it scared the living shit out of me, I think, in precisely the way I needed.

Fever Dream is about environmental disaster and motherhood linking hands in a ghastly but gorgeous way. It is about earthhood. It is a beautiful, singular, slim beast of a novel and I can say a million things about it but I don't want to ruin it for the reader. The thing I will say, the thing that stuck with me, was the way the novel dealt with a desire for something I'd craved my whole life and had only grown exponentially since I'd become a mother – the superpower to be able to prevent a terrible thing from happening.

In the novel's original language of Spanish, the title more closely translates to *rescue distance*. The mother, Amanda, is always trying to calculate the amount of distance that may exist between her and her daughter, Nina, wherein she still has enough time to get to her if something bad happens.

Since my daughter had been born, I'd been trying to calculate the rescue distance every day of our lives but didn't have the words for it. When I woke up hungover, I felt like I'd thrown my notion of rescue out the window. I felt like a terrible mother. But after reading *Fever Dream*, I newly felt like now I had the tools to understand in a way that I hadn't before what my role was and how different my role was from what I thought it should be. It is a book that feels hopeless and yet provides hope. AKA:

This can happen but it has not happened yet.

We can still save each other. We just need to read more, and listen more, and hear more, and love more. And hate less. Read more, to hate less. And start with this book. It is the kind that provides life experience like a primer, and it's beautiful and sad, and like all sad things that are also beautiful, it is also full of hope. The same hope I had that morning when I swore I would never wake up a hungover mother again. At least not on hot sake, that's for sure.

Lisa Taddeo is a journalist, novelist, screenwriter and author of non-fiction and short stories. Best known for her work of non-fiction, Three Women, which won a British Book Award and which she is adapting for TV, she has also written a novel, Animal, *and a short story collection,* Ghost Lover. *She has written for numerous literary magazines and is a two-time recipient of the Pushcart Prize.*

Meena Kandasamy

on *The God of Small Things* by Arundhati Roy

The God of Small Things came to us in tiny doses.

First, we read in the papers that a young Indian woman was bringing home the Booker Prize. I was a 13-year-old teenager in Chennai (Madras) in 1997, and her win was a welcome change for us from the other achievements that routinely bombarded us from the newspapers – an Indian woman won Miss World, an Indian Woman won Miss Universe. For geeky-nerdy girls like me, Arundhati Roy was a beacon of hope and a welcome validation: Indian women could do other things than take part in beauty contests.

The second time, Arundhati Roy was sued for obscenity for *The God of Small Things* – and this only made my resolve to read the novel even greater.

The third time, many months after it was released, I held a physical copy of this book when it was ordered for our school library. I cajoled the librarian to let me take it home for a night. I remember reading it with awe, with admiration, with tears in my eyes. I went to school the next day having finished the book, never having slept a wink, and I could not stop talking about it to all my girlfriends.

We all took turns reading it. Something even more beautiful transpired: we would sit around in a circle on our school desks and take turns reading its loveliest pages aloud. I remember reading aloud the last chapter ('Cost of Living'), I remember the lovers coming together for a midnight tryst, I remember the lines, 'Biology designed the dance. Terror timed it', I remember the beautiful way the novel ends on a Malayalam word (*naaley*, which means tomorrow) that the lovers tell each other.

This was a book that made promises. This was a book that kept them.

This was a book that made me feel that one could do something magical with language. This novel made and unmade language for me. Everything about this book felt like perfection when I first read it as a teenager; everything about it feels like perfection when I reread it now.

For all of the ornate, lyrical writing, for all of the sentence cadences that made one's heart stop-jump, it is an extremely political text. It is a novel of place – it captures the paradise-like beauty of Kerala like no other. It is a novel of childhood – no one can write the rebellion within little hearts with the feistiness of Roy. It is a novel of abuse – the abuse of state power, the abuses of feudalism, the predatory abuse of a child by OrangeDrink LemonDrink Man. It is also a novel of immense resistance and great beauty.

Ammu, 31 years old ('a viable, die-able age') when the novel opens, is a heroine like no other, and I appreciate her all the more now that I'm a mother of two small children just like her, and I'm in my thirties, too. Roy wrote of her protagonist: 'She wore flowers in her hair and carried magic secrets in her eyes. She spoke to no one. She spent hours on the riverbank. She smoked cigarettes and had midnight swims.' She was conventional and unconventional at once. It is impossible not to fall in love with such a heroine. It is impossible for such a heroine not to fall in love. And when she falls in love, she transgresses caste and class.

Her story with Velutha (labourer, Untouchable) is the pulsating heart of this novel. Roy writes about caste taboos that enforce endogamy: 'It really began in the days when the Love Laws were made. The laws that lay down who should be loved, and how. And how much.' It is a deceptively simple sentence; it hides the horror that caste codes are capable of committing. Years afterwards, when I visit an atrocity zone like Dharmapuri where hundreds of villages of Dalit (ex-Untouchable) people have been burnt to ashes because of an inter-caste marriage, when I read about the honour-killings of inter-caste couples, I remember the quiet defiance of Roy's protagonists. The love that wrapped Ammu and Velutha together, a love that allowed them to tamper with the Love Laws, a love that is made eternal in her words is a love that is alive even today, and it is a love that is almost always punished with death in my country.

This is a book that will always stay with me. I urge every one of you to pick it up. It will change the way you look at love, at rivers, at beauty, at children, at marriages, at men, at women, at death. It will change the way you look at yourself. It will change the way you want to change the world. Roy breathes life into language in every single sentence.

Meena Kandasamy is an Indian poet, novelist and translator. The author of three novels, including When I Hit You, *which was shortlisted for the 2018 Women's Prize, she has also written two collections of poetry, two essay collections and has translated numerous works from Tamil into English.*

Taiye Selasi

on *Moon Tiger* by Penelope Lively

I have loved books – in a very literal sense – for as long as I can remember; in my earliest memories of myself, at three or four, I am holding one open. By about 15, I knew – beyond a shadow of a doubt, and despite a new interest in kissing – that the greatest pleasures in the world were reading and writing prose. I devoured the books assigned at school, the greatest hits of 19th- and 20th-century literature, and adored so many that I never quite knew how to answer the question of a favourite. Each book I rated held for me as a reader an irreplicable magic: the humour in this one, the poetry in that, the world-building, the word play, the plotting. Victorian classics, Icelandic epics, Nigerian bildungsromans. I read insatiably, indiscriminately. I was, proudly, a promiscuous lover of literature.

Then, at 21, I fell in love. I can't quite remember who gave me the book or suggested that I read it. In retrospect, it seems improbable that I hadn't read it before. What I'll always remember is how it felt to start that book one autumn day, the blue-green cover of the paperback, not heavy in the hands. There was the usual pleasure, the magic aforementioned, but a feeling, too, without precedent: the sense of experiencing a text not as a reader but as a writer. Minutes into those first pages – with their quickly shifting narrators – I knew that I was reading the work of the writer *I* wished to become. If I were to succeed in achieving my childhood dream of becoming a published author, it would be (I vowed) because I'd written a book like this one. As a reader, I have no favourite book. As a writer, I have *Moon Tiger*.

All these years later, all these books later, I have remained utterly faithful. No other novel has ever displaced this touchstone for me as a novelist. Needless to say, Penelope Lively won the 1987 Booker Prize because *Moon Tiger* is a masterpiece. But for me the joy of reading it rested, from the start, on something more intimate than admiration. Curious, the intimacy: *Moon Tiger* tells the story of an upper-class Englishwoman (Claudia), of her brother, lovers and daughter (in order of importance), of wartime Egypt. None of the novel's content aligns with any part of my life. I didn't 'see myself' in the story; rather, I found myself in the telling.

The *way* that Lively tells her story told me that I'd been had, that the rules of 'good writing' (as I had been taught them) were *not* sacrosanct, that the walls built around 'literary fiction' could be jumped at will. Bouncing back and forth between past tense to present, starting sentences without subjects, ending paragraphs with ellipses, moving from first person subjective to first person omniscient to third person objective and back again: this was the wildest, freest, most thrilling prose I'd ever read. It left me giddy, wondrous. Was writing *allowed* to be so free?! Was a writer?

I'd identified, as a dutiful student, my three favourite features in fiction: repeating motifs (M. Kundera), nonlinear narrative (W. Faulkner), poetic prose (C. McCarthy). But I'd never read one novel that combined all three, and that did so with such apparent ease. I was not naive enough to imagine that writing *Moon Tiger* had been easy for Lively. Rather, I could sense first an easiness about the novel's dazzling structure, the assembly of its disjointed paragraphs, and second the *novelist's* ease with these moving parts – as if Lively had never doubted the structure she'd created, despite its never having existed. The novel seemed to be writing its rules – or better, teaching its reader its rules – as it went along, the unfurling of form as dazzling as the unfolding of content. I read the novel again and again, underlining words I couldn't define at the time (sybaritic, paroxysms), inserting asterisks and exclamation marks (repeats on page 117!), as one studying some ancient text. With almost every sentence I asked myself: How is she making this work? Until one day an answer came. Trust. Lively trusted herself to rewrite the rules, I finally understood. She trusted her talent, yes, but more (and much harder), she trusted her text.

And that she *was* she – not Mr Kundera, Mr Faulkner, Mr McCarthy, with utmost respect to all – but a British woman born in Cairo who lived down the street from me in Oxford? This, in a literal sense too, changed my life. By so obviously believing in her rebellious prose, Lively gave me permission to believe in mine. *Moon Tiger* is the novel that set me on the path to becoming an author – or, more to the point, on the path to authoring wild, disjointed *Ghana Must Go*. I'd always loved books. Only after reading *Moon Tiger* did I know that I could write one. Perhaps all novelists are faithful to one such novel? Not the favourite but the one that sets us free?

Taiye Selasi is a British-American author and photographer of Nigerian and Ghanaian descent. She holds degrees from Yale and Oxford universities, is the author of the much-discussed essay, 'Bye-Bye Babar (Or: What is Afropolitan)', the short story, 'The Sex Lives of African Girls', and the New York Times-*bestselling* Ghana Must Go, *which was published to worldwide acclaim in 2013. A local of many cities, she currently lives in Lisbon.*

Nikesh Shukla

on *The Spider-Man comics* by Marvel

Like kitchens at parties, the back of the comic shop was where you'd find the 'cool' kids. We were the nerds, the ones who traded comic books at school, tried to read everything we could, couldn't afford anything, used our meagre resources to buy issue ones and foil variant covers because they would hopefully make our families fortunes decades later. They didn't, but the richness of that experience found me, in my twenties, still standing at the back of the shop, reading the funnies. Instead of Junaid and Riaz, my childhood accomplices, I would run into the writer Inua Ellams and we'd sit by the stacks reading for an hour silently, before going our separate ways. It's where we forged a lifelong kinship.

Like the rest of the 'cool' kids, I read Spider-Man comics obsessively. It was the mid-1990s and we were in a particularly contentious era for Spidey fans. It started with the introduction of a new symbiote, Carnage, who was more ruthless and terrifying than Venom, and ended with the resurrection of Aunt May, who died during the controversial Clone Saga. It was a pretty heady time to be reading the funny books.

I connected with Spider-Man in a spiritual way. I was Peter Parker. He was me. Maybe I was one of his clones. An Indian version. A Pavitr Prabhakar almost (nerd alert: there *is* an Indian Spidey. His name? Pavitr). This was way before nerd culture became mainstream. When we were the bullied kids, the kids everyone rinsed, the kids who hid, at breaktime, and even at the back of the comic book shop, reading, swinging through friendly neighbourhoods, slinging webs, thwipping the baddies and traversing the multiverse in search of justice. Definitely not the 'cool' kids.

Peter Parker's dual identity – one moment the science nerd, the other as friendly neighbourhood Spider-Man – spoke to me. I empathised with the way he switched between shyness in one life and cockiness in the other. He wore different masks and spoke in different languages, much as I did.

My parents weren't wealthy and the worst thing I could do, in their eyes, was waste money. Comics were a waste of money: specifically, a fiver a week, earned through a paper round, on several issues that took 15 minutes to read, and then five minutes to reread a day later.

The idea of putting on a suit and being a better version of yourself appealed to me. For Superman, putting on the suit entailed being himself (Clark Kent being the everyday mask he wore); for Spider-Man, putting on the suit meant being everything Peter Parker couldn't be. I found comfort in that. In life, I was Peter Parker; reading comics, I was Spider-Man. I dreamed of the confidence with which Spider-Man dispensed of Doctor Octopus or the Green Goblin; the cockiness with which he deployed his web-shooters; the wisecracks he flung at villains with abandon.

'I'm glad you remembered the hyphen,' he told Electro. 'Most people leave it out.'

'Too bad you couldn't get a new hairstyle,' he told Doc Ock.

Comics became a lifeline as I approached my teenage years. Spider-Man lived with the consequences of bad decisions he made. To be in physical danger because of bad decisions, because of the burden of guilt, because of the need to hide your true self, that was me as a teenager.

I lived in fear of being beaten up. Not because there was any real threat of someone knocking me out, but because I was a teenager and I wore my outsider status like a brick wall that I was always on the verge of getting shoved against. Comics allowed me stillness, escapism, a world where quiet nerds like me could make a difference.

The more comics I read, the more I became obsessed with being a writer. I didn't care what: short stories, the great American novel, film scripts, arcs for comics, raps. I wasn't fussy.

My first, terrible attempts at writing were synopses for Spider-Man arcs that were yet to be written. Thankfully, this juvenilia no longer exist because when I moved out of home with my girlfriend at 22, I decided I could no longer have ties to such childishness. I threw it all away. I think back to what those issues taught me about storytelling, how they gave me the tools to pace, to ensure that dialogue is punchy, exciting, realistic and not overwritten.

The biggest thing comics taught me about writing was that bad writing involved characters explaining the plot to each other. Good writing showed you the plot. Writing those synopses, in a brown exercise book, I honed these skills.

I wrote Peter Parker into my school. I made his antagonists my own. I made Mary-Jane a girl he got the train with. I resituated his battles with Sandman and the Vulture in north-west London. Peter Parker became a cypher for me. Spider-Man became the best possible version of myself.

Nikesh Shukla is a British writer of novels and YA fiction, editor of essay collection The Good Immigrant *and co-editor of* The Good Immigrant USA. *A Fellow of the Royal Society of Literature and a member of the Folio Academy, he has also authored a book on writing and a memoir,* Brown Baby: A Memoir Of Race, Family And Home.

Nina Stibbe

on *My Side of the Mountain* by Jean Craighead George

I was eight or nine when my Canadian godmother gave me a copy of *My Side of the Mountain* by Jean Craighead George. Though a good and keen reader, being given books for Christmas at that age always seemed like a missed opportunity for money or sweets or talcum powder. This book was different though. Firstly, none of my vast, book-loving family had read it, or even heard of it, and so, unlike the usual book offerings, it was neither sacred to my mother nor special to an aunt nor cherished by my older sister; it felt like mine. Secondly, the cover struck at the heart of my favourite preoccupations. A boy in ragged clothing stared out at me, a bird of prey on his arm. Beside him, a small kettle on a rudimentary fire let out a wisp of steam. Wild animals in the near distance perfected the scene.

'I ran away to the Catskill Mountains in May. I had a pen knife, a ball of string, I thought that was all I needed,' the narrator told me via the minimal blurb.

My Side of the Mountain is the diary of Sam Gribley, who has left his overcrowded family flat in New York to live in the Catskill Mountains for a year in a hollowed-out tree. He's pretty young, probably 12. Running away from home was a story staple back then, a fact that author Jean Craighead George acknowledges in an introduction to a later edition; 'Be you reader or writer, it is very pleasant to run away in a book.' We loved to fantasise about it but running away in real life was tricky (mainly, back then, because of a lack of resources and the question of where to?). I once forced one of my brothers to run away with me; he wasn't keen, but I didn't want to go alone. I packed a bag of snacks but soon got fed up with his inability to commit to the adventure or enjoy himself. My sister and I did manage to camp out for a night in a horse trailer, but in truth no one really cared, it was the 1970s – a time of benign neglect, and we discovered that without handwringing from parents, running away is no fun.

The diary opens in deepest winter, when Sam really believes he might be snowed in or freeze to death. We know he'll survive (otherwise how did he write the rest of the diary?), but it is terrifically exciting and compelling, and the first-person narrative is informal and candid and feels modern and very American. I remember thinking it brave of this boy to admit feeling frightened. Rereading as an adult, it occurred to me that this is, of course, a woman's version of a boy and therefore we get to see his frailty. Far from implying innate survival instincts, he describes numerous failings and mistakes, like struggling to get his flint to spark, even though a Chinese man in New York has taught him. And when he becomes unwell, he hikes down the mountain to research nutrition in the library. It really does show someone learning to be independent in a methodical and rational way.

The book is sweet, but it's also quite brutal. There are elements of Peter Rabbit; the anthropomorphising and befriending of wild animals and making acorn pancakes and herb tea, but soon he's stolen a baby hawk from its nest and trained it to kill rabbits for him, which he roasts and eats, especially enjoying the liver. He traps a deer and, though we're spared the gutting of it, he does make a trouser suit from deer hide. Again, he gives us the rough with the smooth; on the plus side, he has a deer-skin suit but then when he wears it for his walk to the library, he gets a bit teased by a townsperson. It's really a delightful

127

balance. He has a beloved racoon neighbour and again, he resists presenting the racoon as cuddly or friendly, in fact the racoon never really likes him and is either stealing his acorn stash or attacking his ankles. I loved that things don't always go right for him, and he is able to accept that racoon for who (s)he is.

I bought this book for Sam and Will Frears, who I was a nanny for in the 1980s, and I mention it in my book, *Love, Nina*. Will enjoyed it, because he liked adventure, but Sam asked me to read it quickly to get it over with. I guess I overhyped it. I've adored this book for 50 years. It influenced my reading for certain. I think it taught me how transportive books could be. It also taught me tolerance, as a person, and reduced my expectations of woodland experiences. Whenever I can, I foist second-hand copies onto people, but I don't know anyone who has loved it as much as I do.

Nina Stibbe is a British author and screenwriter, best known for Love, Nina, *which was adapted into a BBC series, starring Helena Bonham-Carter. The author of six novels, including the most recent,* One Day I Shall Astonish The World, *she has been awarded a Comedy Women in Print Prize and the Wodehouse Prize for comic fiction.*

Ruth Ozeki

on *The Pillow Book by Sei Shōnagon*

When I was 12 and getting curious about sex, I found a copy of *The Pillow Book of Sei Shōnagon* on my mother's bookshelf. I knew the book couldn't possibly be sexy, or racy, or even romantic; my Japanese mother wasn't any of those things. She was a linguist, and most of her tomes were thick Asian-language dictionaries, dense with tiny ideograms on tissue-thin pages.

But this book, with its suggestive title, was different. It was old, with a torn paper book jacket that hung askew, like a kimono falling off a shoulder. When I pulled it from the shelf, the jacket tore a bit more, revealing boards of beautiful Japanese paper, printed in a pattern of red and blue. Afraid of damaging it further, I was about to put it back, when a sentence on the cover caught my eye:

Nearly a thousand years ago this book was written by a woman who was equally famous for her wit, her poetry and her lovers.

…um, Mom?

I took the book to my bedroom to read under the covers and found myself flung back a millennium into the Heian Court of 10th-century Japan. The translation I was reading, by Arthur Waley, was published in 1928. Waley translated only the parts of Sei Shōnagon's book that interested him, about one-quarter of the original work. The rest was his exoticised commentary on her life, about which little is known. She was born around CE 966. Her father was a provincial official, a scholar and a poet. She served as a lady-in-waiting to the Empress Teishi. She may have been married. She may have had a child. After the Empress died, she disappeared from history. Legend has it that she died in poverty, alone.

The Pillow Book, which she wrote during her 10 years at court, is a genre-bending miscellany of lists, reminiscences, fashion tips, aristocratic intrigue and gossip. She claimed she was writing it for her own amusement and professed dismay when a visitor filched and circulated her manuscript, but her sincerity is questionable. Even through Waley's bowdlerised, Orientalist lens, this was a woman writing with authority and an awareness of her audience – which most certainly did not include a 12-year-old girl in America, a thousand years later, reading in bed with a flashlight.

I was looking for a role model (other than my mother), and I found one in this arch, acerbic, intelligent contrarian, with strong opinions and an uncompromising voice. Although a stickler for etiquette, Sei Shōnagon freely broke gender taboos by using 'men's Japanese' and quoting Chinese poetry. Her exquisitely refined taste made her a discerning connoisseur. If she were alive now and on TikTok, she would be an influencer. Influenced, I took her words to heart.

'The success of a lover depends greatly on his method of departure,' she wrote. 'To begin with, he ought not to be too ready to get up, but should require a little coaxing: "Come, it is past daybreak. You don't want to be found here . . ." and so on.' She scorns the lover who pulls on his trousers too quickly, fumbles around in the half-darkness for a misplaced fan or wallet, bumps into things and mutters to himself, fusses with his robes, 'so that when he finally takes his departure, instead of experiencing the feelings of regret proper to such an occasion, one merely feels irritated at his clumsiness'.

When I finally grew up and had lovers of my own, I would recall this thousand-year-old piece of wisdom.

But what moved me and inspired me most were her lists. Sei Shōnagon created taxonomies that appealed to my awkward, alienated pre-teen self, and like Waley, I picked the ones that interested me, copying them assiduously in my diary: Annoying Things; Deceptive Things; Embarrassing Things; and Things that Give Me an Uncomfortable Feeling.

Later, in high school, I found a newer, more complete English translation by Ivan Morris, which included more lists: Rare Things; Squalid Things; People who Seem to Suffer; Times when One Should be on One's Guard; Things that Make the Heart Beat Faster.

The Pillow Book contains over 150 lists, and from them, I learned an important lesson: make interesting lists. Your taxonomies will change how you experience your life. If you only make lists of things you must do, then you'll only do the things you must. If you make lists of Things that Make the Heart Beat Faster, your heart will beat faster.

Like a guiding spirit, Sei Shōnagon's influence in my life continued. In graduate school, I studied her original text in classical Japanese. Later, when I started writing fiction, her montage-like, genre-bending approach inspired mine. When I wrote my first novel, *My Year of Meats*, about a documentary filmmaker with a strong contrarian streak, Sei Shōnagon floated into the story.

Some 50 years after I first found *The Pillow Book*, a new translation by Meredith McKinney was published. As I started to read, my heart beat faster. Would I recognise my old mentor? Would her words still move me, her lists still inspire? I needn't have worried. This newest translation is the best yet, an Outstandingly Splendid Thing that brings Sei Shōnagon vividly to life for new readers, including perhaps another 12-year-old, in search of meaningful taxonomies.

Ruth Ozeki is a Canadian-American author, filmmaker and Zen Buddhist priest. She is the author of four novels and one autobiography. Her 2013 novel, A Tale For Time Being, *was shortlisted for the Booker Prize, while her 2021 novel,* The Book of Form and Emptiness, *won the 2022 Women's Prize for Fiction. She teaches Creative Writing at Smith College in Massachusetts.*

Elizabeth Day

on *The Murder of Roger Ackroyd* by Agatha Christie

When I was 12, I discovered Agatha Christie. I can't remember who first gave me a copy of one of her books, but I can distinctly recall the thrill of reading them. I loved her pacy plots, written with a straightforward flair that even a child could grasp. I loved Hercule Poirot and his insistence on breakfast toast that had to be made from a square loaf, accompanied by eggs matching in size. I loved Miss Marple for constantly subverting people's assumptions that she was nothing more than a benign little old lady. But most of all, I loved the clarity with which Christie's chaotic fictional world of murder and infidelity and disputed inheritances restored itself by the final page, as if the Earth itself were resting back on its axis with a reassuring certainty.

Perhaps it's no coincidence that I came to the books when I was looking for stability in my own life. I was an English child who had moved at the age of four to Northern Ireland with her family. It was a province beset with violence and civil tension, where to speak with an English accent (as I did) was to mark you out as an occupier or, worse, an enemy. The daily drive to my primary school was interrupted by military checkpoints manned by soldiers with machine guns. Saturday trips to the local shopping centre were frequently shut down by bomb scares. Every August, balaclavaed men marched in the streets. Once, in Belfast, I walked through the city the day after a massive explosion. The pavements were lined by mangled cars and my feet crunched against shattered glass. I got used to news of people being killed. Most of the time, their killers weren't caught.

Unlike the real world, I knew when I picked up an Agatha Christie book, that the murderers in these pages would always get their just deserts. In fact, I became so enamoured with Christie that I used to give each novel of hers I read a mark out of ten and a short two-line review on sheets of foolscap I tied together with string. I was a harsh critic: only two of her books ever got full marks. One was *And Then There Were None*. The other was *The Murder of Roger Ackroyd*.

The reason I've chosen to write about the latter is because it is the one that has had the most direct influence on my own writing. The edition I read was found in a second-hand bookshop. It had a blue cover, and the pages were tinged with that specific ochre colour that suggests decades of different fingertips and library shelves. I felt extremely grown-up having such a book in my possession. The cover didn't even have a picture on it, which seemed like the acme of sophistication.

The plot of *The Murder of Roger Ackroyd* starts out as classic Christie: an attractive widow dies from an overdose of veronal, followed a day later by the man she was meant to marry – the eponymous Roger Ackroyd. Hercule Poirot is summoned. His 'little grey cells' are perplexed, but of course he solves the case, and it becomes one of the most startling conclusions of his illustrious career.

Because *The Murder of Roger Ackroyd* contains a twist. A twist of such epic narrative proportions that any time I have written an unreliable narrator since (and there have been a few), I aim to pull the rug from underneath the reader with the same shocking brilliance that Christie did for 12-year-old me.

I have never forgotten the immense satisfaction Christie's masterstroke gave me. It was the perfect twist because I guessed it just before it happened.

The realisation dawned literally a page or two ahead of the big reveal, and it made me realise that sometimes guessing the twist at the right time can be just as satisfying a reading experience as not sussing it out at all. It makes the reader feel in on the secret, but without sacrificing the white-knuckle ride it has taken to get there.

Agatha Christie might never have won a grand literary prize but her lasting commercial appeal – she is the bestselling novelist of all time, behind only Shakespeare and the Bible in terms of sales – is profoundly inspiring to me. She knew what it was to put the reader at the centre of all her storytelling, without using self-consciously literary language or pretension. Yes, some of her writing is notably dated and contains derogatory stereotypes of race and ethnicity. But for a woman of little formal education, born into the tail end of the 19th century, who taught herself to write against the constraints of her time, to achieve what she did is remarkable.

As entertaining as her books are, her life was one of her most impressively executed plots. I remain in awe of her for both.

Elizabeth Day is a British journalist, novelist and broadcaster. A former features writer and columnist, she has written four novels including Magpie *and two works of non-fiction including* How To Fail, *based on her hit podcast of the same name. She also presents Radio 4's* Open Book *and* Sky Arts Book Club Live. *She has won a Betty Trask Award, a British Podcast Award and a British Press Award.*

Caleb Azumah Nelson

on *NW* by Zadie Smith

The first semester of university is always such a strange time. Everything feels like it's changing and shifting around you. Books were always the place where I could retreat when I wasn't quite sure about things and so, my first semester at Coventry, I spent a lot of time in the bookshop. I was a big reader at school, and my teachers were always yammering at me to try Zadie Smith. So, one day in the bookshop, I picked up *NW*. Less than a decade later, I think I've read this book 20 times.

NW represented a big shift in my reading. Until that point, aside from Malorie Blackman, who also lived in south-east London like me, I hadn't read any fiction in which I had seen myself represented or seen people that I really knew. *The Times* used to do this promotion when I was 10 or 11, where you could take a token to WHSmith and get a Penguin classic. I spent most of my time working slowly through the classics. But I was always really intrigued as to where the characters who looked like me, sounded like me, were.

NW is about four people whose lives intersect, set in north-west London. It's billed as experimental fiction. I think Zadie Smith does things in it that border on genius. It was the first book that I read that used the European way of denoting speech, that used a little dash as opposed to speech marks, which really evokes this sense of intimacy. The characters felt so close and well rendered and complex. There was a sense of humanity that ran through them. This ability for them to be beautiful and messy. This enormous sense of warmth. I would not have written my first book, *Open Water*, if I hadn't read it.

I have a pristine, signed copy of *NW* and then a copy that I actually read. I met Zadie Smith at an awards ceremony a few months ago. She approached me and spoke to me about *Open Water*, like I was a contemporary. I asked her if she'd seen that I use a quote from *NW* as the epigraph:

> There was an inevitability around their road towards one another, which encouraged meandering along the route.

Your words open the novel, I said. She waved it away.

After I read *NW*, I read her books in order: *White Teeth*, *Autograph Man*, *On Beauty*. I did the same thing when I discovered James Baldwin and Toni Morrison, where I doled out the writing, reading each book as closely as possible. I found something in each of them. *White Teeth* has a real energy to it, and it's so big and sprawling and incredibly ambitious. I would find myself laughing out loud. *On Beauty* feels like the best writing to me, the most classical kind of British novel. I love Zadie Smith's essays, too. Her voice is so clear in her non-fiction. There's an essay in one of her older collections, called 'Joy'. I'd never had the language for this feeling before. Joy is such a mix of so many big and terrifying emotions. I remember finding that essay and printing it off and carrying it around in my bag, every so often pulling it out to read. Joy is about being present in your life. But of all her work, *NW* is still my favourite: the characters, the humanity, the experimentation, the playfulness.

The first draft of *Open Water* was a car crash. I was trying to take the parts of *NW* and render it my own. It didn't work. The relationship between the two texts needed to be subtler: about energy and feeling and the page. *NW* is so confident. Someone who has put her feet on the ground and said, I am writing this novel. *NW* is so good at building a world out of a world that already exists. This rendering of a specific place was something that I really wanted to do for south-east London. In *Open Water*, south-east London is its own character. People want to be invested in communities, particularly after the pandemic. Making a small world within a world is the way to do it.

I knew as soon as I read *NW*, that I would be returning. Each instance that I have returned to the text, something has appeared that I didn't notice the first time round. There's a feeling of joy when I return to her work, as something new unravels and unspools over time. It's like speaking to a friend every couple of months. You know that each time you visit, you're deepening the knowledge that you have of them. Reading, for me, not only deepens the knowledge that a writer has of a text, but of myself. It encourages me to look not just outwards but also inwards.

Caleb Azumah Nelson is a British-Ghanaian photographer and the author of Open Water, *which won the 2021 Costa Book Award for First Novel, was shortlisted for the Waterstones Book of the Year and longlisted for the Desmond Elliott Prize.*

Kit de Waal

on *The Thing About December*
by Donal Ryan

When I first read *The Thing About December* by Donal Ryan, I felt sick with jealousy. I was horrified that someone had written something so fantastic. It was really one of those moments that I just thought, why am I bothering? And then I thought okay, *this* is the craft. *This* has to be the standard.

The book is about a vulnerable, sheltered young man called Johnsey, who lives in rural Ireland, in 2001. When his parents both die within six months of each other, he inherits this farm, which is on a very valuable piece of land, and the developers and other farmers soon come circling. It's almost a thriller, in that you cannot stop turning the page and you're terrified about what's going to happen. There's an enormous amount of heart in it – Johnsey just wants to be loved. The use of language is also so poetic. I don't mean poetic in the Byron sense; I just don't get poetry, quite frankly. I mean phrases that you will never have heard before.

One of the things that drew me to *The Thing About December* is it was from the point of view of this vulnerable young man, like my own book, *My Name Is Leon*, which came out in 2016. The territory was very similar. There was something about the way he had chosen to tell this devastating story that really showed me the way. It is a great thing to aim for, I think, to try and emulate your heroes. I have a whole shelf in my study of books that I can reach for when I am trying to accomplish something. There's *City of Bohane* by Kevin Barry, *The Heart of the Matter* by Graham Greene, *The First Bad Man* by Miranda July and *The Haunting of Hill House* by Shirley Jackson. It's a very disparate collection of books. There might be one thing about the book that the author does very well that means their book is on the shelf. With Donal Ryan, there are so many things he does well. He's the only author with all his books on the shelf.

I read a great deal, but I didn't start reading for enjoyment until my early twenties. I was brought up as a Jehovah's Witness, where I had to read the Bible all the time. I wasn't interested in books; I thought they were for swots. My sister read a

lot; she was a goody-goody. I left the church at
16 and had a few years of drinking and taking
drugs. I was not in a good place. I started reading
to get me out of my own head. I began with the
classics – *Les Misérables, Madame Bovary, The Riddle
of the Sands, War and Peace*. All the monsters. I'd
start with Flaubert and then I'd read loads of
French literature in translation. I'd see that
Flaubert knew Arnold Bennett, so then I'd read
all of him. And then I'd see he knew Somerset
Maugham, so it was over to him next. I didn't
read a contemporary book for 15 years.

Now, I listen to a lot of audiobooks and,
at the moment, I enjoy a lot of memoir and
autobiography. I read indiscriminately and
without snobbery. This idea that every book
has to say something profound about the world
is rubbish. The only thing a book has to do is
whatever the reader wants it to. The only thing
that's changed in my reading habits over the years
is that now, if I don't like a book, I don't force
myself to finish it. Life's too short!

I now know Donal Ryan well. I am an adjunct
professor of creative writing at Limerick, and he
works there too. I once gave a talk, and he did
the introduction and he was so complimentary
about my work that I wanted to go up to him
afterwards and ask him for his notes to keep.

I remember thinking, *Donal Ryan thinks I'm a good writer!* It really was one of the best moments in the world. He is the nicest, most humble writer you will ever meet – he wears his genius so lightly. My favourite passage from *The Thing About December* is this: 'Mother always said that January is a lovely month. Everything starts over again in the new year. The visitors are all finished with and you don't see sight nor hear sound of them until next Christmas, with the help of God. Before you know it, you will see a stretch in the evenings.' It's a very Irish thing to say. It has a sense of hope. The winter is over, and we are on the turn into something better.

Kit De Waal is a British-Irish writer. Her 2016 debut novel, My Name Is Leon, *was shortlisted for the British Book Awards, the Costa Book Awards and the Desmond Elliott Prize. The founder of the Big Book Weekend and a creative writing scholarship at Birkbeck, she has also written numerous short stories and a memoir,* Without Warning and Only Sometimes.

Deborah Levy

on *I Capture The Castle* by Dodie Smith

I Capture The Castle is about an eccentric family who live in a wreck of a castle in Suffolk in the 1930s. They are completely broke and take it in turns to bathe in a tin tub overlooking the fields. In summer, they swim in the moat that circles the castle.

I was 13 when I first read Dodie Smith's magical novel. How I would have loved to swim in that moat, too. In fact, in my imagination, I have swum in it many times. I suppose the point of reading at any age is that one life is not enough. Books can give us many more lives to live. The most exciting event of my week, aged 13, was when the ice-cream van, Mister Whippy, turned up on our road on Fridays. Obviously, living in a castle rather than a flat in the suburbs of London, and not having parents who made us hoover the carpets and do our homework, seemed like a more exciting life.

The story is brilliantly told from the point of view of 17-year-old Cassandra Mortmain. She wants to capture everyday castle life in her diary and writes in it every day for a year. She has much to tell us about her hopes, fears and big feelings. Her older sister, Rose, is a stunning beauty. Cassandra is supposed to be the brainy one. Do we think that sort of binary is really true? The kind and attractive handyman, Stephen, is deeply in love with Cassandra. They are about the same age. He saves up to buy her a radio and dreams of kissing her in the bluebell wood. She is not sure she returns his feelings and gives these complications an airing in her diary. Meanwhile, gorgeous Rose yearns for nice clothes and romance. Their cute little brother is a bit of a nerd and good at maths. Unfortunately, their mother died when they were young.

Their father is a bad-tempered writer who is very stuck in his life. He once wrote a famous book but doesn't seem to be able to write another one to support his family. In fact, he has not written a word for 12 years and lives in the tower of the castle, seething, selfish and sad. We are supposed to believe he is a genius. He did however have enough charm to persuade a young, spirited artist called Topaz to marry him. So, the siblings have a stepmother who likes to walk naked in the fields to summon inspiration for her paintings. When the book starts, Topaz has had to sell off the furniture to buy food.

How are they going to survive?

Everything changes when the landlords of the castle, two wealthy Americans, Simon Cotton and his brother, Neil, arrive in Suffolk. Rose is determined to marry one of them and sets about making Simon fall in love with her. She thinks the way to go about this is to play the piano (badly) and sing old-fashioned songs. She wears ridiculous long dresses (dyed a weird colour by Topaz) and tries to act as if she were in a Jane Austen novel. The truth is she doesn't have a clue. After all, Rose has grown up in a castle and has not been educated at school. She does her best to appear sophisticated and irresistible. She faints, she flirts. After a few mishaps, it works. Reader, she almost marries him.

A wedding is being arranged. Rose now has lovely dresses and perfumes, a new chic hairstyle and stylish shoes. She wants to marry into money to save her family from poverty. Indeed, a giant juicy ham is sent to the castle by the Cotton family. Does Rose love Simon Cotton? Does it matter?

It does matter to Cassandra. She is confused about her own feelings for the brothers – no spoilers here. Before the summer ends, she has had her first kiss (passion) and her second kiss (not so sure about this one) and two offers of marriage. She declines both of them.

Perhaps these young women would have been better off getting a job picking fruit in the fields or working in the café at the railway station. To be honest, that possibility didn't occur to me when I was 13. I just wanted to know what was going to happen next. Cassandra does something extreme (helped by her adorable little brother) to get her father to write again. They sort of succeed.

It was clear to me that it was Cassandra who was going to become a writer, which was her ambition all along. It was secretly my desire too. I was inspired and enchanted by this most unusual novel. What a relief it was, at 13, not to be talked down to in a book, no moralising, no being told to eat my vegetables or to have an early night. The best books are not about flawless people without problems. By the time I got to the last page, I decided to keep a diary, just like Cassandra did. In fact, I was often writing in this diary when Mister Whippy's ice-cream van arrived on our road on Fridays. I would hide my new diary under the bed and make a dash for the ice-cream called a '99', with a flake stuck in its soft, swirling centre.

Deborah Levy is the author of Swimming Home, Hot Milk *and* The Man Who Saw Everything – *all three nominated for the Booker Prize. Within Levy's acclaimed trilogy of living autobiographies,* Things I Don't Want to Know *and* The Cost of Living *were awarded the Femina Prize 2020 in France, while* Real Estate *won The Christopher Isherwood Prize 2022 for Autobiographical Prose in the US. Deborah Levy is a fellow of the Royal Society of Literature.*

Damon Galgut

on *Train Dreams* by Denis Johnson

I heard Denis Johnson's name a few times before
I gave him a try. I think I started with *Angels*, his
first novel: a really wonderful book. So is *Jesus'
Son*, a collection of linked stories about addiction
and rehab, clearly territory Johnson knew well.
But neither of these comes close to the experience
of reading *Train Dreams*, a crystalline novella that
first appeared in 2002. I've returned to it a few
times over the years, and it never fails to move and
thrill me, but the occasion I first read it has stayed
with me in a profound way.

It's hard to explain exactly why it works,
because it's about a nobody, and nothing of great
significance happens to him. Robert Grainer is
a labourer in the American West. It opens with
a scene of arbitrary violence in 1917 and jumps
around to other arbitrary scenes from his life,
from childhood all the way to his death in 1968.
The closest he comes to a meaningful connection

is when he acquires a wife and child, but he loses them both in a fire. He's devastated for a while but goes on because he has no choice. Mostly his life is shaped by the railroads, through work and travel, but that's the only shape to any of it. He's not by any means a heroic figure. He has no mission to fulfil.

This is how Johnson describes him after he dies:

He'd never been drunk. He'd never
purchased a firearm or spoken into a
telephone. He'd ridden on trains regularly,
many times in automobiles, and once on an
aircraft. During the last decade of his life, he
watched television whenever he was in town.
He had no idea who his parents might have
been, and he left no heirs behind him.

I think of Cormac McCarthy every time I read Johnson, but especially with this book. There are some similarities in their prose, though Johnson doesn't go in much for heavy rhetoric. But the plotlessness of *Train Dreams* is reminiscent of *Suttree*, where a lack of plot is actually the point. Things happen, then other things follow. In *Suttree*, the aimless drift of life is embodied by the river; in *Train Dreams*, it's the railway that connects all the episodes together.

As an addict, Johnson was familiar with the edges of society and the human creatures that inhabit it. There's no end to the crooked tales he could dream up; his weakest novels tend to get buried in febrile, drug-driven imaginings. But *Train Dreams* is strange in a completely different way. Because it's actually a historical piece, he has the scope to imagine some of the weirder fringe types living on what was still a kind of frontier. There's no big overarching story, but there are multiple small stories along the way. Johnson writes great dialogue, and at least one conversation (between Grainer and a man who's been shot by his own dog) extracted a belly laugh from me.

Grainer lives his early years in that time when the world is changing for ever – when the industrial age is about to break, but myth and the supernatural are still part of the language of life. He sees the spirit of his dead wife one night. Then his long-lost daughter visits him in the form of an injured wolf-woman. These events are presented as natural and real because that's how Grainer experiences them.

All of this is odd and interesting and at times deeply moving. But the true pleasure of this book is its style – dryly lyrical, but also highly restrained. The reach of the story is, in fact, epic, but it's told with the most glancing of touches. There's something wonderful in the way Johnson leaps, in a sentence, 'years later, many decades later, in fact . . .' On the one hand, you've got the pain of life and the heaviness of history; on the other hand, it's being related with the lightest puff of air.

And then he pulls a genius move at the very end. I wouldn't want to spoil it for anyone, and it only makes sense as the conclusion of a certain trajectory … but the last scene does another little hop in time, back to what could have been one more arbitrary moment, but isn't. Johnson creates a perfect symbol for the historical epoch he's writing about and pulls together all the little shards and fragments into one image. It's heartbreaking and mystical, and it keeps coming back to haunt me.

Damon Galgut is a South African novelist whose first book was published when he was just 17. His ninth novel, The Promise, *won the Booker Prize in 2021 – a prize for which his 2003 novel,* The Good Doctor, *and his 2010 novel,* In a Strange Room, *were both shortlisted. He has also written several plays.*

Naoise Dolan

on *Schott's Original Miscellany*
by Ben Schott

When I'm writing fiction, the first thing I have to do is make the characters talk. It's awkward, meeting strangers. I'll spend five minutes deciding if X person says 'Hi' or 'Hello'. Then something clicks. I'll still have to decide how everyone looks and what the weather's doing. But once the characters speak, there's a story. Dialogue is my passion. I can't believe I'm paid to write it. I'd do it anyway; I'd be a sad sack if I never made the heads talk. That need has been in me nearly all my life. Nearly, but not quite. And it started with the page in *Schott's Original Miscellany* listing U and non-U English.

I was a 12-year-old in Dublin when I read the miscellany. Most books I 'happened on' as a kid now show up on Google as having been smoking-hot publishing sensations. As was *Schott's*. It's a salutary check on the old authorial ego to reflect on the juggernauts you'd considered weird little things. The cover might say that it's a *Sunday Times* bestseller, but a 12-year-old won't see that. I was my best self when I was 12. I didn't care about status – mine or the writer's. Our minds met. I learned what I could. *Schott's Original Miscellany*, a book of selected trivia from many fields of study, seemed to me then a map of endeavour. Seek what you want, cherish what you find, but remember there'll always be more.

Whatever your specialism, *Schott's* grants it no particular prestige. There's no hierarchy of knowledge. Clothing care, law, medicine, bagpipes: it's all just stuff among stuff in a world that's stuffed with stuff. Even at 12, I found some entries obvious. Why was he telling us things everyone knows in between things nobody possibly could? But my humdrum was different to the next person's.

It's impossible to dislike the miscellany. If you're truly determined to hate things, then you might find it boring. But it reminds you on every page that life holds more than you can ever comprehend. Being okay with Earth's hugeness is one thing you need as a fiction writer. We are all just small in the scheme of it. That's joyous. There's no meaningful starting point in a universe so vast. Pick one and go. That's what the miscellany taught me: peaceably moving through infinity.

Why I was particularly keen on the U and non-U English part of the miscellany is because it taught me language-neutrality. Until I read it, I'd often wondered: 'Why does the language around me seem different to the language in books?' – which is to say, 'Why do I think Ireland and Irish people are un-literary?' I'd grown up on *Anne of Green Gables* and Enid Blyton and there wasn't much Irishness in those.

Seeing the U/non-U thing awakened my perception for a writer's main job, gathering language. I began reading more Irish writers with the mindset that there's no better or worse English, there's just usage. My dad makes brilliant sentences when he talks. He's a funny, inventive, well-spoken Irishman with no literary ambition whatsoever and he's just as much a source to me as Dickens. (If anyone fears 'no literary ambition' is harsh on Mr Dolan, please know he's fundamentally an Irish dad, and he'll be glad I've informed the public that my own notions aren't contagious.)

The U/non-U thing also taught me that the meaning of a word doesn't come from the sounds. 'Pardon?' is the harder one to remember. It's relatively context-specific, whereas 'What?' has broader uses so stays on the tip of your tongue. Also, there are more 'What?'-sayers. The working-and upper-class 'What?' bloc outsizes the 'Pardon?' club by far. We could all decide to say 'green' instead of 'Pardon?' and 'red' instead of 'What?', and so long as everyone got the memo – one pities the traffic-light engineer on birthday leave – those noises would then carry the meaning.

There's no material law dictating that if you say 'Par' and then 'don', you must buy everything in John Lewis. (Which is a joke I know how to make because the U/non-U entry also made me wonder what different people in England are stereotyped as doing. I only gathered data once I moved to England aged 24, but the table kicked it off. The miscellany keeps giving.)

You can't look at class differences as a child and find dignity. When you're an Irish 12-year-old your main takeaway is going to be that it's silly and fun and just words. With this starting world-neutrality, I gleaned from all sources. A fiction writer's process is therefore less one of talking aloud than of scrapbooking key elements like Schott does. Style needn't be terse – you can write beautiful flowing sentences – but if you want them to be loved and shared, then each must be a self-complete miscellany.

Choose your corner, the miscellany says. That's what I took from it as a girl. Choose your corner since any will delight you – and keep visiting other people in theirs.

Naoise Dolan is an Irish journalist and novelist, best known for her debut novel Exciting Times, *which was longlisted for the 2021 Dylan Thomas Prize, the Women's Prize for Fiction and Waterstones Book of the Year.*

William Boyd

on *Catch-22* by Joseph Heller

The years of Nigeria's bitter and devastating civil war, the so-called Biafran War of 1967–1970, during which more than one million people died, coincided with my late teens. I was 18 in 1970. I was born in Ghana and initially educated there until, in 1962, my father, a doctor, moved the family from Ghana to Nigeria. By this time, my secondary education was taking place at a boarding school in Scotland, and I returned to Nigeria in the school holidays. Despite my background and my periodic enforced absence, I unreflectingly felt that West Africa was, in almost every sense, my real home.

The onset of the civil war in 1967 changed the conditions of our lives in Nigeria in dramatic and, sometimes, irritating ways. Power cuts and water shortages were normal. Armed soldiers were visible everywhere. You were routinely stopped at roadblocks and searched. Guns were pointed at you. Every night the television news bulletins provided graphic illustration of the brutal fighting as the Nigerian army pushed into the shrinking secessionist enclave that was Biafra. The Nigerian episodes of my life began to punctuate my normal school career like surreal dreams. I was once strip-searched by soldiers at Lagos airport who suspected me of carrying drugs. Our neighbours dug a slit-trench in their back garden. My father and I were almost fired upon by drunken militia when we inadvertently drove through their flimsy roadblock. Our cook, Israel, on a visit to his home-village, was forcibly conscripted into the Biafran army but managed to desert and return to us. As I flew out to Nigeria from London – the overnight flight lasted about eight hours in those days – I had no idea what strange adventures would be awaiting me on my holidays from school.

It was my habit in my late teens to fly luggage-less, for some reason. Everything I needed I carried in my pockets – toothbrush, money, passport, ticket, reading matter. This meant I moved through customs at Lagos airport with ease and no delay. Thus unimpeded, I was then quickly able to catch a connecting domestic flight to Ibadan, in Western Nigeria, where my parents lived.

In 1969, at Heathrow, waiting to board the flight to Lagos, I realised I had nothing to read. In an airport bookstall I bought the first book I saw that intrigued me. It was *Catch-22* by Joseph Heller. The paperback cover showed an American airman standing in the middle of a runway, staring out and shaking his fist vengefully skywards. I knew nothing about the book, but the blurb told me it was a war novel, set in Italy in World War II. There was no inflight entertainment on planes in those days. If you wanted to pass the time you read a book.

After take-off, I started reading *Catch-22* and read on throughout the night. I was utterly rapt, utterly held and read the book in one long blast of mesmerised absorption. I'm sure that trance-like concentration was a consequence of my own experience of living in a war-torn country. Heller's absurdist vision of war and combat and the helpless impotence of his protagonists chimed very closely with what I had witnessed and understood. Until the Biafran War began, my experience of warfare was one derived entirely from movies and novels. What I was living through in Nigeria, however, was absolutely nothing like what I had read and seen at the cinema and on television. Subjectively, unconsciously, I was becoming aware that conventional dramatised and fictionalised versions of war were at a remote distance from the real thing – the real thing that I was seeing as I looked about me. And then I read *Catch-22*.

It was an intense, though half-reasoned, intellectual experience for me. For the first time I found in this fiction a clear identification with what I was experiencing in Nigeria. I saw how a novel could – through humour, absurdity, tone of voice and unhinged imagination – capture the weird contingencies of the world I was inhabiting in Nigeria. I saw how an artist – a novelist, in this instance – could replicate life's textures and reality in a way that no journalism, documentary or history could. I was beginning to comprehend, I now realise, the unnerving power of fiction.

I don't think I can say that my fervid, night-long 1969 reading of *Catch-22* on board that aircraft made me want to be a novelist – I was too young and too callow for that transformation to occur – but it did change my reading habits. I now actively sought out fiction that authenticated my experience – or experiences that I was curious about – and judged that fiction by the paradoxical standards of veracity that *Catch-22* had established, as far as I was concerned. And I suppose that change, that new awareness, did set me off on the path I was eventually to follow.

Twelve years later, I actually wrote my own war novel, *An Ice-Cream War*, and almost everything in that novel originated in or was informed by what I'd experienced in Nigeria and the Damascene moment when I opened *Catch-22* and started reading.

William Boyd is a Scottish writer and screenwriter. The author of 17 novels, including Restless *and* Any Human Heart *(both of which he later adapted for screen), and five short story collections, he has won numerous literary prizes.*

Emma Dabiri

on *Quicksand* by Nella Larsen

The first time I read *Quicksand* by Nella Larsen, I didn't love it. I didn't even particularly like it. I felt a bit *meh*, in truth. Twelve years later, at the age of 40, I read it again and I thought, Oh my God! This is incredible! I had a completely different response to it the second time round. I was shocked by how many parallels existed between me and the protagonist. And that fascinated me. That a book I could feel so ambivalent about could touch me so personally a decade later. It showed me the importance of rereading. I now teach it, as an example of the Harlem Renaissance.

The book is about Helga Crane, a Black American 18-year-old living in segregated America in the 1920s. Helga has a white Danish mother and a Black Caribbean father and when her father dies, she is sent away to a historically Black university in the South. It's the beginning of her journey through various different cities in the world, trying to find where she belongs, never being fully permitted a place of her own. As a result of the trauma of not being allowed to live with her family and being sent away when her father dies, Helga is a prickly, brittle character. She travels through all these different spaces, desperate to be loved, making decisions that only alienate people, while acting imperiously and defensively.

Quicksand is not straightforwardly autobiographical, but it is drawn from Nella Larsen's life. She also had a white mother and a Black father and was sent away to university. She was very critical of what she considered the hypocrisies and contradictions of the Black American elite, and in the book she makes very thinly veiled references to people and places who were prominent in Black society at that time. The university that Helga attends is thought to be based on Tuskegee University in Alabama, a historic Black university that Larsen was sent to. Ostensibly a place for Black advancement, Helga finds this institution to be full of snobbery that mimics white upper-class values. After she graduates, Helga moves to Harlem and initially, she thinks that she has found her people in this bohemian scene of Black writers and artists and poets. But soon she starts to see the same tendencies and hypocrisies – and so she flees to her distant relatives in Copenhagen.

Denmark is entirely white as a place, but it has no racial segregation and initially, Helga finds relief. But then she realises that she is being exoticised by her aunt and uncle, who are dressing her up and parading her round the city, using her as a tool to increase their social standing. She yearns for America and so she returns and – in a slightly bonkers twist – marries a rural pastor and relocates to the South. She has loads of children and … still doesn't feel like she fits in. You sense the pattern, here.

The book does not offer Helga a resolution. It's actually pretty depressing. But it's also iconic – a slim modernist classic that condenses so much complexity about race and class and gender into such an economy of words. When my students were reading this recently, they were really shocked that it was written 100 years ago. It feels so 'now'. It's incredible that it was Larsen's first book – the writing is sublime.

Sadly, after just two books, and a failed third attempt, Larsen stopped writing. She became a nurse and died in obscurity. Both *Quicksand* and *Passing*, her second book, which has recently been made into a film, had a good critical reception when they came out, but were then lost until the

1980s, when they were rediscovered and crowned canonical texts, thanks to the efforts of Black American scholars. They are now better known than they ever were in Larsen's lifetime.

That early experience of being from a place but not being able to claim it is something I felt strongly. I wasn't born in the 1920s and I wasn't rejected by my family, but I lived in Ireland where there was this constant refrain of being told that I didn't belong, that I was not Irish. I had spent the first four years of my life in Atlanta, which I saw as this distant, Black utopia and the first chance I had to go back, as a teenager, I did. It was my first time in predominantly Black spaces since I was very young and I had expected to feel this sense of belonging, but it didn't happen. This time, I *looked* like the people around me, but culturally I was so different. I was so Irish!

That sense of searching for a place that is mine, where I feel like I belong, has followed me until quite recently. I'm currently writing the proposal for my third book in New York City, and this space feels like mine. I moved to Margate with my family recently and I feel like it's where I'm meant to be now. But maybe it's because I haven't been there for that long. Maybe, like Helga, I'll feel the pull in a little while. Maybe this is how it goes.

Emma Dabiri is an Irish journalist, broadcaster and academic. The author of two works of non-fiction, Don't Touch My Hair *and* What White People Can Do Next, *she is currently the Heimbold Chair of Irish Studies, a researcher at Goldsmiths, University of London and an associate at SOAS. She has presented numerous series across television and radio for the BBC.*

Fatima Bhutto

on *her bookshelf*

The act of reading is a sacrament. A holy practice. But like all sacred things, it is easy to lose sight of the wonder. I remember the first moment that I knew I was a reader – the first time that I lost myself in a book. It was during school; I was in third or fourth grade at the time and we had been given quiet time to read at our desks. One moment there was time and the next it had vanished. Nothing existed between me and the pages of the story – no worries, no fears, no needs or longings. I was never the same again. But to choose a single book as a gateway into this extraordinary world of timelessness, no pain and pure being – the only nirvana any of us can possibly hope to achieve – would be impossible. It can't be done. One has to see books as portals, as offerings sent to us exactly when we need them the most.

When I first learnt how to read, I read everything: street signs, food packets, the slender writing on my father's cigarette packs – they had no health warnings in the 1980s and so narratively didn't offer much. I graduated to Nancy Drew, the R. L. Stine horror books and the innocent fantasies of the girls at Sweet Valley High. But as I got older and life turned more fraught, more dangerous and more lonely, that's when I began to receive the offerings.

After my father was killed, the elementary school librarian at our school, whose son was the same age as my brother, six years old, gave me *Tiger Eyes* by Judy Blume. It told the story of a 15-year-old girl struggling in the aftermath of her father's unexpected death. I was one year younger than the girl in the book. I read it in my father's bedroom, in the near dark, and cried through the chapters. When I returned to school, an English teacher gave me *Ordinary People* by Judith Guest, a novel about a family coping with trauma and loss, better known for having been turned into an Oscar-winning film. I don't remember if we read the novel as a class or if the teacher gave the book only to me. But I remember feeling understood, for the first time, during my loneliest season of grief.

Whenever I weathered a crisis, somehow there was a book to meet me; a story, an author, a writer who managed to soothe and tend to me in quiet ways. *To Kill A Mockingbird* was another English class read that prepared our young, hopeful hearts for the unfairness of the world. Only a book can do that without breaking you. But it wasn't just sadness that books offered shelter from; there were books for those hours where we cannot but be alone: *What You Have Heard is True* by Carolyn Forché, a stunning memoir about the poet's time in El Salvador before the start of its bloody civil war, *This House of Grief* by Helen Garner, the greatest book about a modern trial that I can think of, *The Shapeless Unease* by Samantha Harvey, a moving and funny book about insomnia. Anyone with a broken heart would thank God for *Bluets* by Maggie Nelson and just about anything by James Baldwin. When I was writing and stuck, Rachel Kushner's novels breathed life and awe back into me. When I was writing my last novel, *In a Free State* by V. S. Naipaul and a short story by Colm Tóibín taught me how to think of it in a radically different way (Cormac McCarthy's *The Road* made me want to write it in the first place).

There is no one book that saves a life – the truth is much more profound. We are such fragile, complex things. What are people made of but memories of each other and stories that tether us to the world? Those simple stories – our first kiss, our last kiss, our guilt, our longings, sombre moments, celebrations, humiliations, illnesses – are the only things that will survive us. 'Still, what I want in my life is to be willing to be dazzled,' the poet Mary Oliver wrote, 'to cast aside the weight of facts and maybe even to float a little above this difficult world.' It's stories that will remain long after we and our puny troubles are gone, circulating in the ether, passed on to loved ones, told and retold until they crumble, becoming dust, until one day someone notices a grain somewhere and stops to look.

Fatima Bhutto was born in Kabul, Afghanistan and grew up in Syria and Pakistan. She is the author of six books of fiction and non-fiction, including The Shadow of the Crescent Moon, *which was longlisted in 2014 for the Bailey's Women's Prize for Fiction. Her most recent books are* The Runaways, *a novel, and* New Kings of the World, *a reportage on globalisation and popular culture.*

Acknowledgements

A huge thank you first and foremost to our contributing authors, who have inspired me and so many others with their work. Thank you to the National Literacy Trust for their tireless work in children's literacy and to Bloomsbury, particularly Alexis Kirschbaum, Stephanie Rathbone, Emilie Chambeyron, Lauren Whybrow and Akua Boateng, for generously supporting this charitable venture. Thank you to Charlie Greig for your help assembling the puzzle pieces, David Mann for the book's beautiful design, and Nelle Andrew, always, for your support. And thank you to my mother, who made me into the bookworm I am today, for the bi-weekly library trips and the stocking full of books. I hope that my children will always feel as supported in their reading, as I did by you.

A Note on the Editor

Pandora Sykes is a journalist and broadcaster. She is the creator of multiple podcasts and audio documentaries including *The High Low*, and is the host of *The Missing*. Her debut essay collection *How Do We Know We're Doing It Right?* was a *Sunday Times* bestseller, and she has written for the *Sunday Times*, *Vogue*, *Guardian*, *GQ* and *Elle*. She lives in London.

A Note on the Type

The text of this book is set in Baskerville, a typeface named after John Baskerville of Birmingham (1706–1775). The original punches cut by him still survive. His widow sold them to Beaumarchais, from where they passed through several French foundries to Deberney & Peignot in Paris, before finding their way to Cambridge University Press.

Baskerville was the first of the 'transitional romans' between the softer and rounder calligraphic Old Face and the 'Modern' sharp-tooled Bodoni. It does not look very different to the Old Face, but the thick and thin strokes are more crisply defined and the serifs on lower-case letters are closer to the horizontal with the stress nearer the vertical. The R in some sizes has the eighteenth-century curled tail, the lower case w has no middle serif and the lower case g has an open tail and a curled ear.